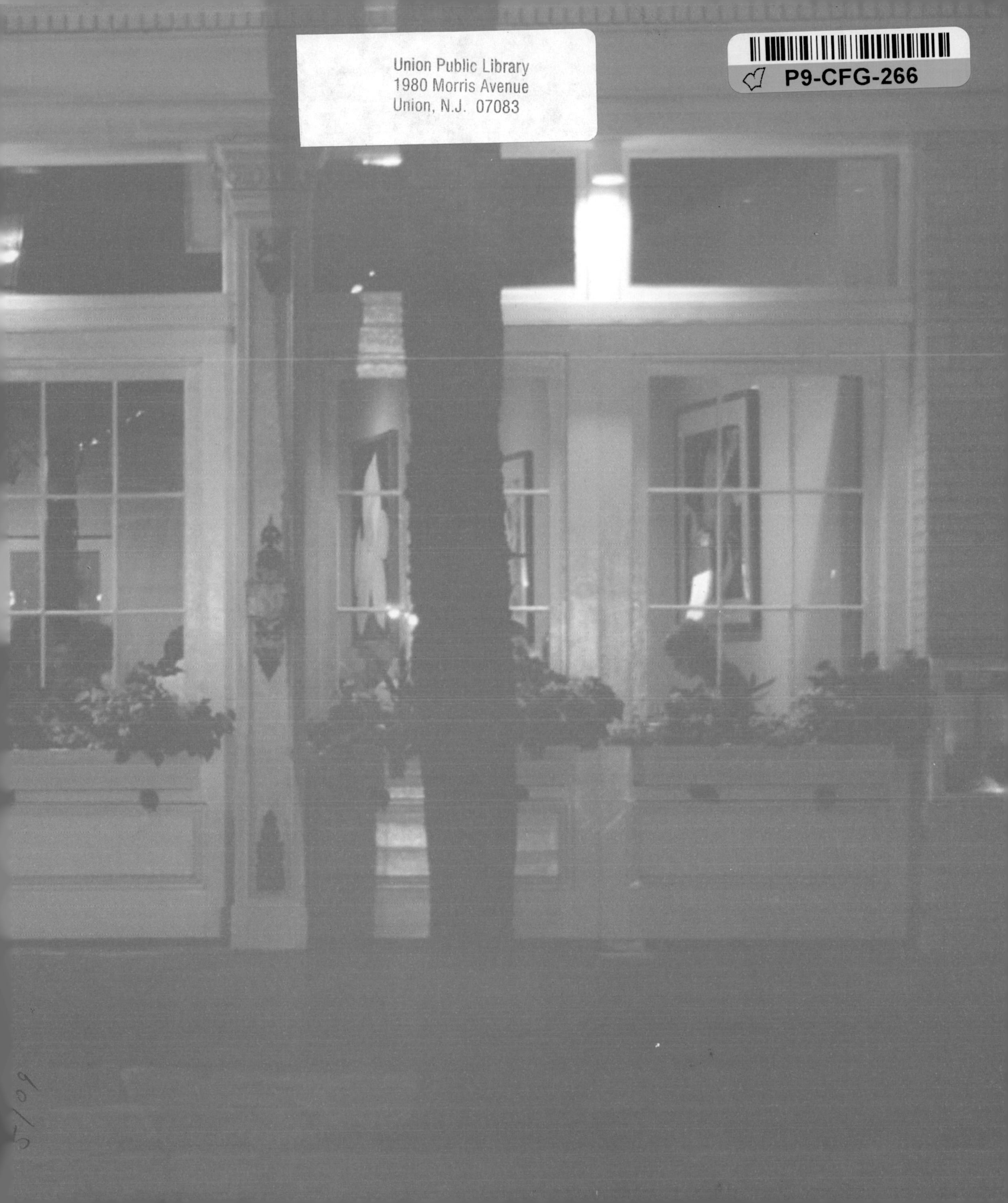

Magnolias

Magnolias

Authentic Southern Cuisine

Donald Barickman

Photographs by Rick McKee

Gibbs Smith, Publisher

TO ENRICH AND INSPIRE HUMANKIND

Salt Lake City | Charleston | Santa Fe | Santa Barbara

First Edition
10 09 08   8 7 6 5 4

Text © 2006 Hospitality Management Group, Inc.
Photographs © 2006 Rick McKee

Published by
Gibbs Smith, Publisher
P.O. Box 667
Layton, Utah 84041

1.800.748.5439 orders
www.gibbs-smith.com

Designed by Kurt Wahlner
Printed and bound in China

Library of Congress Cataloging-in-Publication Data

Barickman, Donald, 1962-
Magnolias : authentic Southern cuisine / Donald Barickman ; photographs by Rick McKee.— 1st ed.
     p. cm.
A sequel to: Magnolias southern cuisine. 1995.
Includes bibliographical references and index.
ISBN 10: 0-941711-87-0 (alk. paper) ; ISBN 13: 978-0-941711-87-6
1. Cookery, American—Southern style. I. Barickman, Donald, 1962- Magnolias southern cuisine. II. Title.
TX715.2.S68B365 2006
641.5'975—dc22
                              2005033904

Contents

Soups and Salads

Blue Crab Bisque 62

Creamy Tomato Bisque with Lump Crabmeat and Chiffonade of Fresh Basil 63

Potato, Leek, and Roasted Garlic Soup with Creek Shrimp and Tomato Chive Salsa 64

Cajun Clam Chowder 66

Elwood's Ham Chowder 68

Black Bean Chili with Scallion-and-Cilantro Sour Cream 70

Shrimp and Rice Salad with Lemon, Garlic, and Dill Vinaigrette 73

Red Potato and Parsley Salad 75

Summer Tomato and Vidalia Onion Salad 76

Arugula Salad with Creamy Goat Cheese,
Roasted Peppers, and Roasted Garlic Vinaigrette 78

Iceberg Salad with Buttermilk, Basil, and Blue Cheese Dressing,
Carolina Ham Cracklings, and Grape Tomatoes 81

Warm Sea Scallop Salad with Lime Dressing Over Boston Lettuce 82

Classic Caesar Salad 84

Mixed Greens with Lemon Herb Vinaigrette 86

Lemon Lingonberry Vinaigrette 87

Tomato Herb Vinaigrette 87

Buttermilk, Basil, and Blue Cheese Dressing 88

Carolina Peanut Vinaigrette 89

Southern Sides

Classic Potato Fries 92

Butter-Whipped Potatoes 93

Parsley Potatoes 94

Carolina Aromatic Rice 95

Red Rice 96

Dirty Rice 97

Baked Blue Cheese and Macaroni 98

Baked Macaroni and Cheddar Cheese 100

Creamed Corn 101

Magnolias' Collard Greens 102

Lady Peas, White Hall Peas, Black-Eyed Peas, Zipper Peas, and Butter Beans 103

Slow-Cooked Okra and Tomatoes 104

South Carolina Hoppin' John 106

Black Beans and Carolina Aromatic Rice 107

Foreword

When Donald called and asked me to write the foreword for his new cookbook, I stopped to collect my thoughts. This was a big deal!

Magnolias, the restaurant on which the book is based, holds a special place in my heart. Not only was it the first real restaurant I worked in as a culinary student, it was my first opportunity to work up-close and personal with a part of American culinary history.

In the late 1980s a revolution happened across the country. Educated young chefs moved outside the world of stodgy, classic French cooking and started looking in their own backyards for inspiration, flavors, and traditions.

Donald was at the forefront of this revolution. He put Charleston, South Carolina on the map as a culinary destination with the opening of Magnolias Uptown/Down South in 1990. At that time, regional American cuisine was being defined by chefs like Emeril Lagasse of New Orleans, Norman Van Aken of Miami, and Jasper White of Boston. Donald's name became part of that list. His imaginative, bold flavors are the definition of Southern cooking. He has proudly carried the torch of true Southern food for over fifteen years.

Donald, along with his business partner Tom Parsell, put shrimp and grits on a white tablecloth with a glass of California Chardonnay and not only created lowcountry cuisine, but created a movement. The city of Charleston has held her head high ever since.

He's a genius in the kitchen, as buttoned up and professional as he is passionate. Donald embraces the lowcountry, the bounty of farmers, the marshlands, and the Atlantic Ocean. They embrace him back.

He loves his restaurants, his staff, and imparting his knowledge to hungry young chefs. I can attest to what a fantastic teacher he is. I grew up on Southern food, but learned how to make it delicious while studying in his kitchen.

If you love big, fluffy biscuits, golden-fried buttermilk chicken, macaroni & cheese, shrimp & grits that will make you cry, black-eyed peas, dirty rice, slow cooked pork shoulder, collards that cook all day with ham hocks, and crab cakes with tomato gravy, then you'll salivate reading and cooking from this book.

Donald is the real deal. His food is flavorful and unforgettable. His restaurants (Magnolias, Blossom, and Cypress) are American institutions. Donald's shrimp and grits will never let this Southern boy forget where he came from.

—Tyler Florence
New York City

Meats and Poultry

Southern Sweets

Grits and Gravies

Skillet-Seared Yellow Grits Cakes 110

Creamy White Grits with Carolina Country Ham and Red-Eye Gravy 112

Magnolias' Spicy Shrimp, Sausage, and Tasso Gravy over Creamy White Grits 114

Shellfish with Lobster Sauce over Creamy White Grits 117

Pan-Fried Grits Cakes with Sautéed Shrimp, Leeks, and Tomato Gravy 121

Pimiento Cheese Grits with Pepper-Seared Sea Scallops and Red Pepper Sauce 125

Grilled Salmon Fillet with Dill Butter over Creamy White Grits 127

Chicken Gravy 129

Fish and Shellfish

Iron-Skillet Crispy Flounder with Lemon Caper Aïoli 132

Blue Crabs 135

Sautéed Grouper with Artichoke and Creamy Crabmeat over
Sautéed Spinach with Lemon and Leek Butter 136

Coriander-Seared Tuna Fillet with Jalapeño and Mango
Vinaigrette, Pan-Fried Potato Cakes, and Sautéed Escarole 141

Fire-Roasted Cedar-Planked Salmon 144

Squash Blossoms with Scallop and Lobster Mousse and Lobster Sauce 146

Seared Tuna Fillets with Carolina Aromatic Rice and
Warm Salad of Artichoke, Lemon, Leek, and Capers 150

Broiled Rock Shrimp with Garlic Butter and Parmesan 153

Carolina Crab Cakes with Tomato Gravy, Creamed Corn, and Sautéed Spinach 154

Buttermilk and Beer Batter–Fried Soft-Shell Crabs 158

Lowcountry Bouillabaisse 161

Introduction

My first cookbook, *Magnolias Southern Cuisine,* was a reflection of the initial success of Magnolias restaurant. This new book was prepared in response to that continued success, and is a celebration of over fifteen years of southern service at Magnolias. When Magnolias opened in 1990, it was one of the first restaurants of its kind in the south. There were a few upscale restaurants, but upscale southern cuisine was a rarely seen concept.

The "Uptown/Down South" theme was inspired by the burgeoning interest in traditional southern dishes taken from the home to a white-table-cloth presentation. Customers seemed ready to appreciate the taste of what has since become known as Carolina Lowcountry cuisine in a more elegant environment. Lowcountry cuisine is a melding of local and regional ingredients with traditional southern staples. The area's lowlands and waterways create an ideal environment for local purveyors to catch seafood and grow lush produce.

As the Founding Chef of Magnolias, I wanted to provide a dining experience that would combine my culinary background in American cuisine, my interest in southern flavors and my growing appreciation for the abundant food resources in Charleston and the Lowcountry. My partner, Thomas J. Parsell, President of Hospitality Management Group, Inc. brought that notion to the table with the establishment of Magnolias. Over the last decade and a half I have worked closely with Executive Chef Don Drake to maintain a standard of excellence in service and cuisine. This standard has carried over into our two other restaurant properties—Blossom and Cypress.

Our properties have become beacons for culinary talent. Over the years, I have had the pleasure of working with accomplished employees, first at Magnolias and then Blossom and Cypress. I am thrilled to have this opportunity to share our most celebrated dishes. We have kept a few much loved originals from my first book, while adding over fifty new recipes.

I invite you to experience southern cuisine in the comfort of your own home. I have tailored each recipe to meet the needs of the domestic chef. Although our restaurants feature Lowcountry ingredients, each recipe can easily be prepared with items found at your local grocer or specialty food store. If you would like to use some of the specific items referenced, I have also provided a resource list. I hope you will enjoy the culinary journey in these pages and also come to Charleston and dine with me.

—Donald M. Barickman
Founding Chef/Partner
Hospitality Management Group, Inc.
Magnolias/Blossom/Cypress

The Southern Pantry

Staple Pantry Ingredients

Stone-Ground Grits: Since the early days of Magnolias, we have used coarse stone-ground white and yellow grits from Falls Mills in Belvidere, Tennessee. The dried white or yellow field corn is processed in a classic grist mill style with a water-driven wheel that powers the millstones that grind the kernels. The ground corn is then sifted into different sizes for use as grits, meal, or flour. I believe that this simple historic staple has made a significant comeback since we started serving them at lunch and dinner seven days a week. Everyone I have come across that has had them has been pleasantly surprised by their texture and natural creaminess and has said that they will never eat grocery-store grits again.

As you may notice in these new recipes, I have changed my way of cooking grits and use no chicken broth. I have learned over the years that the true corn flavor of our grits is brought out best when they are cooked with water and finished with a little bit of cream, butter, and seasoning.

Carolina Ham Trimmings: Salt-cured ham trimmings inspired the creation of Elwood's Ham Chowder the day that I discovered them in a local grocery store. They are created from the trimmings left over from the cured hams, and are now processed into conveniently packaged premium sliced ham. This can be found in the pork section in most Southern grocery stores. In my early days in the kitchen, I remember having to bone out my own hams to use their coveted salt-cured meat; I have the scars to prove it. Today, Magnolias gets its ham pieces from Lee's Sausage Company in Orangeburg, South Carolina.

Tasso: Tasso is created when tender cuts of brined pork are skewered on rods and smoked, then packed in a special spicy rub. The rub almost acts as an additional dry cure that the pork will stay packed in until used. The spice rub on tasso is as valuable as the meat. Try to get all of it incorporated into your dish. Tasso has an endless number of uses in gravies, soups, pastas, and rice dishes, just to mention a few.

Applewood-Smoked Bacon: The applewood-smoked bacon that comes from the Nueske's smokehouse in Wisconsin is some of the best bacon that I have ever eaten. It has great flavor and a unique cured ham quality. Nueske's also has a line of cured and smoked pork products that are all blue-ribbon quality.

Carolina Plantation Aromatic Rice: I made this rice a staple at Magnolias shortly after I met Campbell and Meredith Coxe. They had just started to grow the heirloom Della variety in small amounts and asked me to try it out. I was immediately hooked by its aromatic qualities and the fact that it is the only rice produced entirely in South Carolina in retail quantity. I had not used Carolina Plantation Aromatic Rice prior to the publication of the original Magnolias Southern Cuisine, but you will find it in many of the new recipes. Carolina Plantation also grows and mills their own white and yellow corn grits, brown rice, rice flour, and cowpeas.

Converted Rice: Before I discovered Carolina Plantation Aromatic Rice, my recipes called for converted rice. It is prepared by soaking and steaming brown rice under pressure to transfer some of the water-soluble nutrients into the starchy endosperm. It is then dried and milled as harvested rice would be. The result is a cooked rice that holds its whole grain shape after cooking.

Aluminum-Free Baking Powder: Aluminum-free baking powder does not contain any sodium aluminum sulfate, which is usually found in double-acting baking powders. The sodium aluminum sulfate can impart an offensive metallic flavor that may ruin a dish. I don't know of many people who taste baking powder before it is used; therefore, you only taste the offensive metallic flavor after the product is baked. I recommend Rumford baking powder, which is made by Clabber Girl and is aluminum-free.

White Lily Flour: I have used White Lily since the early 90s and have it on hand at all times. My baked goods would not be the same without it. Made from soft winter wheat, it has less gluten and makes for light and delicate biscuits and pastries.

Salt: When I first started to cook, salt was salt. This is not the case anymore! When I graduated from iodized salt to kosher salt back in the mid-80s, I thought that was it. Now there are so many varieties available, you could start a collection. These varieties range from Celtic sea salt to fleur de sel to black salt, Hawaiian salt, smoked salt, etc. These add great flavor and are worth the elevated prices because most are hand-harvested and imported. Just use some coarse sea salt and freshly ground pepper on beef, fish, chicken, pork, and lamb, and you will notice how they bring out the true flavor. I also use fine sea salt; you will notice it sprinkled throughout my recipes. A good rule to remember about salt is that you can always add more if needed. So, as you season to taste, do not add too much at once as it cannot be taken away.

Butter: Like salts, all butters are not the same. Basically, the difference depends on which formula the dairy is selling you. Less expensive butter usually has more water worked into the batch, which means that you're not really getting butter cheaper, you're getting cheaper butter. These days, the closest to the real thing is the European-style butter you find in upscale grocery stores. This butter also has not been robbed of its butterfat, which is what gives butter its reputation as the king of the kitchen. I determine which butter I'm using when I decide what dish I am going to cook. If I am baking or making brown butter sauces, a Hollandaise-based sauce, or compound butters, I like to use a salted sweet cream version. The salt aids in browning when baking and it also helps a brown butter sauce to have a nuttier flavor and brown color throughout.

Light Olive Oil: You will see light olive oil on the grocery store shelf, but in the Magnolias kitchen, light olive oil is a blend of olive oil and canola oil, usually with a higher percentage of the canola. It has a very neutral flavor and is great to sauté, pan-fry and sear in.

Extra-Virgin Olive Oil: The finest of all olive oils comes from the first cold stone pressing of the olives. It is called extra-virgin and has a dark green color and fruity flavor. I rarely use it as a cooking medium, but I like to finish dishes with it. It is great for a last minute drizzle over tomatoes, salads, meats, and cheeses, or mixed into a dressing. Store it in a cool, dark area to preserve its color and flavor.

Garlic: Always use fresh garlic; the bottled, pre-processed garlic is not the same. I think that some people buy the processed so that they can scoop it out with a spoon and never have to get the pungent garlic oils on their fingers. But a quick fix to rid yourself of garlic essence on your hands is to simply rinse your fingers under cold water while rubbing a stainless object such as the stainless knife blade you used to chop the garlic. There is some magic here. You'll be surprised. An easy way to peel garlic is simply to give a fresh clove a quick crush with the side of a knife and the skin of the clove will just lift off. The smashed clove will only need a little chopping after this process.

Staple Pantry Recipes

Chicken Broth

This broth is extensively used throughout the book and in our restaurant. It produces the flavor base for many of my recipes. I don't know how today's chefs could do without it. We use it like water. If only we could have it piped in!

Makes 1$\frac{1}{2}$ quarts

2$\frac{1}{2}$ pounds	chicken backs, rinsed with cold water
1$\frac{1}{2}$ cups	roughly chopped yellow onion
1 cup	roughly chopped carrot
1 cup	roughly chopped celery stalks, but no leaves
4	large cloves garlic, roughly chopped
2	bay leaves
8	sprigs fresh thyme, or $\frac{1}{2}$ teaspoon dried thyme
10	parsley stems
6	cracked peppercorns
16 cups	water (1 gallon)

Combine all of the ingredients in a large stockpot and slowly bring them to a simmer over medium-high heat. Reduce the heat to low and cook slowly, uncovered, for 2$\frac{1}{2}$ hours. Skim off any foam that may appear and discard. Strain off the broth and place immediately into an ice bath to cool. Discard the bones and vegetables.

Store the broth in the refrigerator, preferably in a clear container in order to differentiate the broth from the sediment of proteins, which will gradually settle on the bottom. Pour the broth off slowly to separate the clear broth from the sediment. Discard the sediment. When the broth has been chilled, it is easy to remove the fat from it. The fat will rise to the top and you can lift it off with a spoon.

The broth will keep for several days in the refrigerator or for several months in the freezer.

Yellow Corn Relish

For Fresh Corn Kernels: Place ice cubes in a bowl of cold water and set aside. Drop fresh corn on the cob into boiling water and cook for 8 minutes. Drain the corn. Rinse with cold water and immerse in the ice water to stop the cooking. Drain and pat dry. Cut the kernels off of the cob by slicing off with a sharp knife.

Makes 3 cups

2 cups	fresh yellow corn kernels (about 4 ears)
1/4 cup	diced red onions, chopped in 1/4-inch dice
1/2 cup	thinly sliced scallions
1 teaspoon	chopped garlic
1/4 cup	diced red pepper, chopped in 1/4-inch dice
2 teaspoons	stemmed, seeded, and finely minced jalapeño pepper
1 tablespoon	chopped cilantro
5 tablespoons	extra-virgin olive oil
3 tablespoons	cider vinegar
1/2 teaspoon	cumin
1/2 teaspoon	salt
1/2 teaspoon	freshly ground black pepper

Mix all the ingredients in a bowl and use as needed or put in a storage container with a lid and refrigerate.

Mom's Spicy Mustard

This is a childhood favorite. My mother always had this sweet and spicy mustard in the refrigerator. It is great as a condiment for grilled sausage, as a dip, and is especially good on fried bologna sandwiches. Try it. I think you will like it!

Makes 2 cups

1 cup	Colmans ground yellow mustard
1 cup	white vinegar

Mix well. Refrigerate overnight in a covered bowl.

2	eggs
1 cup	sugar

Remove the mustard mixture from the refrigerator and allow it to come to room temperature. Beat the eggs in a blender. Add the sugar. Blend just until combined. Add the mustard mixture. Blend just until combined.

Cook the mustard in a double boiler until thickened, whisking constantly. Remove from the heat. Cool to room temperature, place in a storage container, cover, and refrigerate until ready to use.

Mom's Spicy Mustard will keep for 3 weeks in the refrigerator.

Magnolias' Everyday Spicy Dry Rub

This rub can be used on pork, beef, chicken, and fish. If you prefer a less spicy version, cut the cayenne pepper in half; if more spicy, increase it by half. Sprinkle it over your main ingredient as you would other seasonings before grilling, broiling, or sautéing. It's good to keep around.

Makes 4 tablespoons

2 teaspoons	granulated garlic powder
1 teaspoon	cumin
3 teaspoons	black pepper
$1/2$ teaspoon	cayenne pepper
2 teaspoons	granulated onion powder
$2^{1}/_{2}$ teaspoons	fine sea salt

Measure and mix the seasonings together. Store in an airtight container or zipper-lock bag.

Sweet and Hot Pork Shoulder and Rib Rub

This particular rub also works well with beef brisket and chicken.

Makes $2/3$ cup

1 tablespoon plus 1 teaspoon	granulated garlic powder
1 tablespoon plus 1 teaspoon	granulated onion powder
2 tablespoons plus 1 teaspoon	coarse sea salt
2 tablespoons plus 1 teaspoon	black pepper
2 teaspoons	cumin
1 teaspoon	cayenne pepper
3 tablespoons	sugar

Mix the seasonings together. Rub heavily onto the meat before cooking it. Store in an airtight container or zipper-lock bag.

Magnolias' Blackening Spice

Spices lose their flavor when they age, so I recommend that you keep the Blackening Spice for no longer than six months.

Makes 1¼ cups

1 teaspoon	black pepper
½ teaspoon	cayenne pepper
½ cup	paprika
1 tablespoon	chili powder
2 tablespoons	granulated garlic powder
1 tablespoon	granulated onion powder
1 tablespoon	dried oregano
1 tablespoon	dried basil
1 tablespoon	dried thyme
1 tablespoon	all-purpose flour
1 tablespoon	cumin
1 tablespoon	salt

Mix all of the ingredients together and store in an airtight container or zipper-lock bag.

Carolina Ham Cracklings

Makes 1 cup

1/2 pound   Carolina Ham Trimmings (see p. 13)

3 tablespoons   light olive oil

Chop the ham trimmings finely by hand or pulse them in batches in a food processor into small pieces. This is best done while the ham is frozen. Because of the curing process, the ham never freezes rock hard.

Place the ham and the oil in a heavy-bottomed pan and bring the heat gradually up to medium, cooking the trimmings slowly to render the ham of most of its fat. Cook the trimmings for 15 to 20 minutes, stirring frequently, or until the ham begins to become somewhat caramelized and is crispy. When you hear it sizzle and crackle, remove the pan from the heat and, using a slotted spoon, move the cracklings onto paper towels to drain and cool. Use immediately or cool to room temperature, place in a storage container, cover, and refrigerate.

White Lily Cream Biscuits

These are the lightest and easiest biscuits to make. The butterfat in the heavy cream is all that is needed to give these biscuits the fat needed to be mouth watering and lighter that air. No need to cut in butter or shortening. Just mix the self-rising flour with cream to make a moist dough, lightly flour, cut, bake, and brush with butter. The biscuits may also be simply cut into squares or diamonds with a knife if preferred. The addition of herbs, spices, or cheese may be added to the biscuit dough for flavored biscuits.

Makes 24 (1-inch) biscuits

2 1/2 cups	White Lily self-rising flour
1 1/2 cups	heavy cream
3 tablespoons	butter, melted

Preheat an oven to 400 degrees.

Place the flour in a mixing bowl. Add the heavy cream and mix with a spoon until it starts to come together and forms a wet sticky dough. Place on a lightly floured surface, lightly flour the top of the dough, and pat or roll it out 1/2-inch thick. Cut the biscuits with a 1-inch biscuit cutter, place on an un-greased baking sheet, and bake until golden brown, 8 to 10 minutes. Remove from the oven, brush with the melted butter, and serve immediately.

Piecrust

Chilling the piecrust dough between steps as indicated allows the gluten to relax and keeps the butter and shortening cold. This helps to ensure a tender crust and to keep the sides from shrinking and slipping down. Patting the dough out into disks about 1 inch thick and 8 inches in diameter with smooth edges helps in rolling out the dough evenly without large splits or tears that may occur on the edges.

Makes 1 (10-inch) crust

12 tablespoons	lightly salted butter
4 tablespoons	vegetable shortening
2 1/2 cups	White Lily all-purpose flour
1/4 teaspoon	salt
3 to 4 tablespoons	ice water

Dice the butter. Measure the shortening. Put the butter and the shortening on a plate and place it in the freezer to firm the shortening and keep the butter cold while you are assembling the other ingredients.

Combine the flour and salt in a bowl. Add the butter and shortening. Cut into the flour either by hand, in a mixer with a paddle, or in a food processor with a steel blade attached, until the butter is completely cut in and is no bigger than small peas. Slowly add the ice water, lightly combining the ingredients. (It is important that you add the water gradually.) Mix until it is just combined and comes together to form a ball with a little molding by hand. Place on a lightly floured surface and pat the dough into a round, thin flat disk, eliminating any creases and smoothing the edges. Wrap the disk in plastic wrap and refrigerate for at least an hour, or until firm.

When you are ready to make the piecrust, roll the dough out on a lightly floured surface. Roll it into an approximate 14-inch circle that is about 1/8 to 3/16 inch thick, giving the dough 1/4 inch turns as you are rolling it so that the thickness remains uniform. Brush off any excess flour. Roll the dough over your rolling pin and lay it into a pie tin. Trim the excess dough, leaving an overhang of about 1 inch, then fold the overhang inward to rest on the rim of the pie tin. Pat crust to fit the tin. Crimp the edges of the crust with 2 fingers and a thumb. Refrigerate for 30 minutes or up to 1 day.

When ready to bake, fill the pie shell with the desired filling and bake at its required temperature and time until the crust is golden and the filling is cooked, about 35 to 40 minutes.

Helpful Hint: If using just as a baked shell, bake the pie shell alone for 15 to 20 minutes at 425 degrees until it is golden all over, rotating it a quarter turn once or twice through the baking process.

Roasted Garlic

This recipe is easily doubled or tripled if you need more roasted garlic.

Makes 6 tablespoons mashed garlic

1/2 cup	whole, peeled garlic cloves
2 tablespoons	light olive oil
	Water as needed
	Salt and pepper to taste

Preheat an oven to 475 degrees.

Place the garlic cloves in a small oven-proof skillet or saucepan. Add the olive oil and enough water to come half way up the sides of the garlic. Add the salt and pepper. Bring the mixture to a boil, then place the pan in the oven for about 20 minutes, or until the water has evaporated and the garlic cloves have taken on a light golden color and have developed a tender starchy texture.

To be able to measure tablespoons or teaspoons of roasted garlic, lightly chop the roasted garlic cloves, mash the garlic, and then measure it. A half cup of peeled cloves yields approximately 6 tablespoons of roasted garlic.

Lowcountry Lemonade

This is great fresh lemonade. If you pour half a glass of lemonade and add half a glass of unsweetened iced tea, you'll make what I like to call Lowcountry Lemonade. I have since learned that this has been Arnold Palmer's favorite for years. It's real satisfying on a hot summer day down South and worth every bit of the squeezing required.

By using the juiced lemon halves in the syrup, lemon flavor will be added from the oils in the rind of the lemon. The lemonade may also be made sweeter with the addition of more lemon syrup. If you do not like pulp in your citrus drinks, the juice can be strained before it is mixed.

Makes 2 quarts

2 cups	lemon juice, fresh squeezed (approximately 12 lemons), reserving 4 halves for the lemon syrup
4 cups	water
2 1/2 cups	lemon syrup
1 to 2 lemons	for garnish

Mix the lemon juice, water, and lemon syrup together. Pour over glasses of ice. Garnish with fresh lemon and serve.

Lemon Syrup

Makes 3 1/4 cups

4	juiced lemon halves
2 1/2 cups	water
2 1/2 cups	sugar

Combine the lemon halves, water, and sugar. Bring to a slow boil until the sugar has dissolved. Remove from the heat and let cool to room temperature.

Grills

Between the restaurants and my home, I use many grills. Which type I use depends upon what I am going to prepare. I like to have a gas grill for convenience and a charcoal grill for flavor and searing with intense high heat. If I want wood-grilled steaks, pork, lamb, chicken, or fish, I will use my charcoal grill, uncovered, with the addition of hardwood pieces for a natural smoky flavor. I will also use it with the cover closed for slow indirect cooking, while smoking at the same time.

A gas grill offers great convenience and can also be used to cook indirectly as well as directly. Many are designed with more than one gas burner. If you place your product over two turned-off burners while using the third one for a heat source, there will be plenty of heat to cook in the low and slow range of 280 to 300 degrees. You may also place a piece of hardwood near this burner so that it smolders and produces an added smoke flavor.

Compound Butters for the Grill

These butters are a quick way to add great flavor varieties to a grilled steak or fish fillets. While sautéed fish and meats have the pan drippings that can easily be turned into a quick sauce, these butters make up for that flavor that cannot be captured while grilling.

Helpful Hint: The butters can be rolled in plastic wrap into a tube that is about 1¼ inches in diameter. Twist the ends to tighten the roll. Work out the air pockets by piercing them with the tip of a knife or toothpick so that the air can escape. Continue to roll and tighten. You can also just place in a container. Place in the refrigerator to chill.

Before using the butters, allow them to warm up nearly to room temperature to slice into medallions or soften and place in a bowl to dollop on the fish or meat.

It is important not to whip the butters as they become brittle and crumble when trying to cut into medallions. It is best to mix by hand. They can be held for weeks in the refrigerator or longer in the freezer if wrapped or airtight. They can always be available for a last minute flavor enhancement.

Green Peppercorn Butter

Recommended to serve with: Beef tenderloin
filets, strip steaks

Makes 1$\frac{1}{2}$ cups

1 teaspoon	light olive oil
$\frac{1}{4}$ cup	minced shallots
4 tablespoons	green peppercorns, lightly crushed
1 cup	salted butter, room temperature
1 teaspoon	coarse sea salt
$\frac{1}{4}$ teaspoon	freshly ground black pepper
2 tablespoons	minced fresh parsley

Heat the oil in a skillet and add the shallots and green peppercorns. Cook lightly
until the shallots are translucent. Remove from the heat and allow the mixture
to cool.

Place the butter in a bowl and add the cooled peppercorn mixture. Add the salt,
black pepper, and parsley. Stir with a spoon or spatula to combine.

Blue Cheese Butter

Recommended to serve with: Beef filets, strip steaks

Makes 1$\frac{1}{2}$ cups

1 cup	salted butter, room temperature
$\frac{1}{4}$ cup	minced shallots
5 ounces	blue cheese
1 tablespoon	minced fresh parsley
1 teaspoon	coarse sea salt
$\frac{1}{2}$ teaspoon	freshly ground black pepper

Place the softened butter in a bowl. Add the remaining ingredients and mix to
combine.

Sun-Dried Tomato and Basil Butter

Recommended to serve with: Wahoo, tuna,
mahi-mahi, swordfish, grouper

Makes 1 1/2 cups

1 cup	salted butter, room temperature
1/4 cup	minced shallots
1/3 cup	minced fresh basil
1/2 cup	chopped sun-dried tomatoes
1 teaspoon	garlic
1 teaspoon	coarse sea salt
1/4 teaspoon	freshly ground black pepper

Place the softened butter in a bowl. Add the remaining ingredients and mix
to combine.

Lemon-Caper and Scallion Butter

Recommended to serve with: Wahoo, tuna,
mahi-mahi, swordfish, grouper

Makes 1 1/2 cups

1 cup	salted butter, room temperature
1/4 cup	chopped capers
1/2 cup	thinly sliced scallions, using entire scallion
1 tablespoon	lemon zest
1 teaspoon	coarse sea salt
1/4 teaspoon	freshly ground black pepper

Place the softened butter in a bowl. Add the remaining ingredients and mix
to combine.

Dill Butter

Recommended to serve with: Salmon, wahoo

   I prefer to use fresh dill, as the dried doesn't really provide the same taste.

Makes 1/2 cup

1/2 pound	unsalted butter, room temperature
1/4 cup	minced shallots
2 tablespoons	chopped fresh dill or 1 tablespoon dried dill weed
1 teaspoon	coarse sea salt
1/2 teaspoon	freshly ground black pepper

Place the softened butter in a bowl. Add the remaining ingredients and mix to combine.

Herb Butter

Recommended to serve with: Pork chops, mahi-mahi, tuna, grouper, swordfish

Makes 1 1/4 cups

1 cup	salted butter, room temperature
1/4 cup	minced shallots
2 tablespoons	minced fresh parsley
2 tablespoons	minced chives
1 tablespoon	minced fresh tarragon
2 tablespoons	minced fresh basil
1 tablespoon	minced fresh thyme
1 teaspoon	coarse sea salt

Place the softened butter in a bowl. Add the remaining ingredients and mix to combine.

Honey Mustard Butter

Recommended to serve with: mahi-mahi

Makes 1 1/2 cups

1 cup	salted butter, room temperature
3 tablespoons	honey
1 tablespoon	whole-grain mustard
1 tablespoon	minced fresh parsley
1 teaspoon	coarse sea salt

Place the softened butter in a bowl. Add the remaining ingredients and mix to combine.

Uptown/
Down South
Starters

Crab Dip

All crabmeat should be picked over to remove any possible remaining shell, but do it gently because you don't want to break up the lumps. Then place the crabmeat in a strainer and press down lightly to extract any extra liquid. This is a great dip, warm or chilled.

Makes 2 cups

1 tablespoon	butter
1 cup	finely minced yellow onion
1 tablespoon	finely minced garlic
2 tablespoons	heavy cream
8 ounces	cream cheese, room temperature
1 pound	lump crabmeat, gently picked over for shell and drained of any liquid
1 teaspoon	chopped parsley
1 teaspoon	chopped basil
1 teaspoon	chopped chives
Dash each	salt, freshly ground black pepper, and cayenne pepper

Heat the butter in a heavy-bottomed saucepan over medium heat. Add the onion and garlic and sauté for 2 minutes, stirring to prevent browning. Add the cream and stir to combine. Add the cream cheese and whisk until melted and the mixture is smooth.

Remove the saucepan from the heat. Place the mixture in a bowl. Cool for 10 minutes at room temperature. Fold in the crabmeat, herbs, and seasonings. Serve immediately or refrigerate and serve chilled. Accompany with Herb Toasts (see p. 39).

Pimiento Cheese

One of my best friends' mother, Alice Marks, made the quintessential Pimiento Cheese. I have never seen her recipe, so this is about as close as I can get to duplicating her "Southern Caviar." I prefer to use the fresh roasted red pepper. It gives enough extra depth and flavor to be worth the 50-minute roasting and peeling process. If you prefer a spicy version, add 1 tablespoon of sautéed minced jalapeño pepper and a few dashes of hot sauce.

Makes 2 1/2 cups

5	large roasted red peppers, peeled, seeded, and chopped (see next page), or 2 1/2 cups jarred diced red pimientos
1 cup	finely chopped stuffed green olives
1 1/4 pounds	New York or Vermont sharp white cheddar cheese, grated
1/4 cup	freshly grated Parmesan cheese
1/4 cup	mayonnaise
1 tablespoon	chopped fresh parsley
1/2 teaspoon	freshly ground black pepper
Dash	cayenne pepper

Combine all of the ingredients in a mixing bowl and mix well. Season to taste with cayenne pepper. Refrigerate until ready to serve.

To Roast Peppers

Thin peppers will have a shorter roasting time. It's preferable to use fresh peppers that look very healthy and have good thick flesh.

Preheat an oven to 500 degrees.

Wash, drain, and dry the peppers. Rub the peppers with olive oil, just to coat them lightly. Place the peppers on a baking sheet and roast them on the top shelf of the oven for about 25 minutes, turning once or twice. The skin should be well blistered and blackened in some places.

Remove the peppers from the oven. Place them in a small bowl and cover tightly with plastic wrap. Let the peppers cool for 10 to 15 minutes. The skin will be become loose and very easy to remove.

 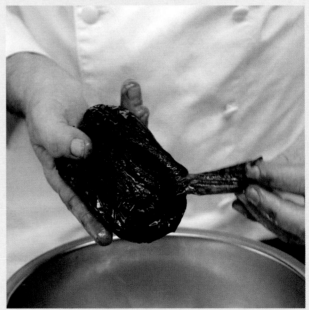

Peel the skin off of the peppers. Remove the stems, cores, and seeds. Do not rinse. At this point you may use the peppers in any manner that you would use jarred pimientos.

Pimiento Cheese and Crab Fondue

This is a pleasant combination of the Pimiento Cheese and the Crab Dip that I happened to blend together on a whim for hors d' oeuvres one evening at the Preservation Society of Charleston's annual book signing. This was a big hit and proved to be a great combination.

Makes 3 1/2 cups

1 recipe	Crab Dip (see p. 34)
1 1/2 cups	Pimiento Cheese recipe (see p. 35)
1 recipe	Herb Toasts (see p. 39)
1 tablespoon	very finely minced basil

Take Crab Dip and fold in Pimiento Cheese. Stir gently until the cheese has melted into the crab dip. Serve warm with the Herb Toasts or your favorite crackers or dipping chips.

Spinach and Artichoke Dip

Makes 3 1/2 cups

3 tablespoons	butter
1/2 cup	minced onion
1 tablespoon plus 1 teaspoon	minced garlic
2 tablespoons	all-purpose flour
1 1/2 cups	heavy cream
3 (10-ounce) packages	frozen spinach, thawed and all liquid pressed out
1 (14-ounce) can	artichoke hearts, drained and cut into 1/2-inch pieces
6 ounces	Havarti or fontina cheese, grated or finely diced
1/2 cup	freshly grated Parmesan cheese
1/4 teaspoon	freshly grated nutmeg
1 1/2 teaspoons	fine sea salt
1/4 teaspoon	white pepper
1/4 teaspoon	freshly ground black pepper
1/4 teaspoon	cayenne pepper

Melt the butter in a saucepan over medium heat. Add the onion and sauté for 2 minutes, stirring to prevent browning. Add the garlic and sauté for 1 minute. Sprinkle the flour over the onion and garlic mixture to make a roux. Stir well to combine and allow to cook over medium-low heat 1 minute more. Add half the cream and stir vigorously until the mixture combines and thickens. Use a spatula to release any of the mixture that may be stuck in the bottom edges of the pan. Add the remaining cream and stir again until the mixture is smooth and thickened. Add the spinach, artichoke hearts, Havarti or fontina cheese, Parmesan, nutmeg, salt, white, black, and cayenne pepper. Continue to stir over medium-low heat until the cheeses have melted. Check seasoning for a balanced flavor. Serve with Herb Toasts (see p. 39).

Herb Toasts

I recommend that you serve this fresh, crisp toast with any of the dips in this
book. The herbed olive oil brushed on the bread gives the toast a mild flavor
and helps it to bake evenly.

3/4 cup	light olive oil
2 teaspoons	mashed garlic
1 tablespoon	very finely minced chives
1 tablespoon	very finely minced basil
1/2 teaspoon	salt
1/2 teaspoon	freshly ground black pepper
1	long loaf of fresh, crusty French bread cut into 1/4-inch-thick slices (or less)

Preheat an oven to 350 degrees.

Combine all of the ingredients except the French bread and let sit for 15 minutes.
Place the slices of bread in a large bowl and drizzle on the oil and herb mixture
as you are tossing the bread slices to coat. Lay the bread slices out on a baking
sheet. Bake for 8 to 10 minutes, or until they are crisply toasted and light
golden in color. Remove from the oven and allow for them to cool to room
temperature before stacking in a basket.

Homemade Potato Chips
with Blue Cheese and Scallions

You can serve these chips as a hors d'oeuvre. Just sprinkle the chips individually, melt the cheese, garnish, and serve on a platter.

Serves 4

1/2 gallon	peanut or canola oil for frying
2 pounds	russet potatoes, washed and sliced 1/16 inch thick
	Fine sea salt
3 to 4 ounces	blue cheese crumbles
3	finely sliced scallions

Preheat the frying oil to 340 degrees.

Using a vegetable slicer or mandoline with an adjustable setting and sharp blade, slice a few chips from a potato to get the thickness correct and consistent. (Consistent size cuts will result in consistent cooking.) Slice all the potato into chips and place into a bowl of cold water. Agitate the chips lightly with your hand to release some of the starch. Drain. Pat the chips with a dry paper towel to dry off any moisture.

Preheat an oven to 300 degrees.

Place about 1/3 of the chips in the fryer with oil, without the basket, gently agitating with a skimmer. It is important not to overcrowd the chips in the oil. Watch over the chips so they cook evenly, around 3 to 4 minutes. The moisture of the chips will slowly cook out and the chips will become crispy and golden. Any under-colored chips may be soggy. Remove the chips from the hot oil with a skimmer, shake off the excess oil, and place on paper towels. Season with salt to taste. Spread out the chips so that they can cool. Do not stack them until they have cooled completely. Repeat this process until all of the chips are fried.

Spread out the chips on a baking sheet and sprinkle with the blue cheese crumbles. Heat in the oven just until the crumbles are heated through. Stack the chips on a plate or platter, sprinkle with scallions, and serve immediately.

Benne Seed Shrimp

with Honey and Hot Chili Sauce

This is another quick and easy way to fry our world-class local shrimp without the big hassle of a three-stage breading processes. A simple dip in the batter and into the hot oil for a quick fry is all it takes. There is no residual flour or cornmeal left in the oil to burn and give the oil an offensive burnt flavor.

Sambal Oelek is a ground fresh chili paste that can usually be found in the Asian section of the grocery store.

Serves 4

1 pound	large shrimp, peeled and deveined
1½ cups	all-purpose flour
1½ cups	cornstarch
2 cups	soda water, chilled
4 tablespoons	black sesame seeds
3 tablespoons	white sesame seeds
2 tablespoons	finely sliced chives
1 tablespoon	chopped fresh parsley
½ gallon	peanut or canola oil
10	cilantro sprigs
1 tablespoon	fine sea salt

Place the shrimp neatly on paper towels and refrigerate until ready to use. They must be free of excessive moisture or the batter may not stick.

Mix the flour and cornstarch together in a large mixing bowl. Add the soda water gradually until it forms a very light, smooth batter the consistency of tempura batter or very light pancake batter. Place the bowl over ice and allow the batter to rest and chill for at least 10 minutes, or up to 1 hour. Add the seeds, the chives and the parsley. Keep the batter very cold, as it is the hot temperature of the oil and the cold temperature of the batter that makes this fried shrimp so crispy and delicate. A few ice cubes may be added directly to the batter just before using to chill it even further. (Just don't get an ice cube in the fryer.)

Preheat the frying oil to 350 degrees.

Practice the technique by dipping the cilantro sprigs in the batter and frying them until crispy, about 1 minute. Place on paper towels.

Pick up the shrimp by the tail two at a time and dip into the batter. Tap them on the side of the bowl to shake off excess batter and gently place them in the hot oil. It is good to hold the shrimp by the tail for a second or two after you put them into the oil just to let the batter start to cook. This is to prevent the wet batter from sticking. For this reason it is best to not use frying baskets. Instead, use a free floating method and a hand skimmer. Move carefully and quickly and fry at least half of the shrimp per batch. This way they cook evenly and after two batches you are ready to serve.

When the batter turns a light golden color and crispy, remove the shrimp carefully from the oil and place them on paper towels. Season the shrimp immediately with the salt. You can keep the shrimp warm in a 200-degree oven while frying the remaining shrimp.

While the shrimp are frying, drizzle the sauce on the plates. Stack the shrimp on the plates and garnish with the fried cilantro leaves. Serve immediately.

Honey and Hot Chili Sauce

2 teaspoons   Sambal Oelek
1/2 cup   honey

Mix together and use for dipping or drizzling around the shrimp.

Spicy Steamed Peel-and-Eat Shrimp

Serves 8 to 10 shrimp lovers

	Water, beer, or a combination of both, $1/2$-inch deep in a large pot
3 pounds	large shrimp
$1/3$ cup	local spice blend or Old Bay seasoning
$1/4$ cup	salted butter, melted
	Cocktail sauce

Heat the liquid until steaming. Sprinkle the shrimp with the seasoning and place them in a steamer basket. Steam the shrimp for 4 to 6 minutes with an occasional stir. They should be nice and pink, with no translucent, raw looking areas. Remove the shrimp from the heat and allow them to cool for a few minutes. Place in a serving dish and serve with the melted butter, cocktail sauce, and additional spice blend, if desired.

Carolina Cup Crackling Oysters

Carolina Cup Oysters are one of our local oysters that have a cup-like bottom shell and a flat top shell. This makes it easier to shuck them and add other ingredients as I do in this recipe. They have the wonderful briny flavor of our local clusters.

Serves 8

6 tablespoons	freshly grated Parmesan cheese, divided
1 cup	mayonnaise
1 teaspoon	Worcestershire sauce
24	Carolina cup oysters, top shell removed, bottom muscle cut, and shell wiped clean of shell pieces and mud
3/4 cup	Carolina Ham Cracklings (see p. 22)
3 cups	rock salt
1	lemon, cut into 8 wedges

Preheat an oven to 400 degrees.

In a small bowl, mix 3 tablespoons of the Parmesan cheese with the mayonnaise and Worcestershire sauce.

Drain most of the liquor off of the oysters. Place about 1 teaspoon of the mayonnaise mixture over the oyster on the half shell. Use a flat knife to fill the topping in around the oyster. Sprinkle the oysters with the ham cracklings and the remaining Parmesan cheese. Place them on a baking sheet.

Place the baking sheet on the upper shelf of the oven and roast the oysters for 8 to 10 minutes, or until the oysters are bubbly and lightly browned. Remove from the oven and allow the oysters to cool for 1 to 2 minutes.

Place 1/2 cup rock salt in each of 8 shallow bowls. Place 3 oysters in each and serve immediately with a small wedge of lemon.

Cornmeal-Fried Oysters

with Jalapeño and Lime Aïoli

I prefer our locally harvested oysters that are smaller size and have a nice briny flavor. They can be found in our seafood markets during oyster season. Otherwise, a small amount of buttermilk and/or hot sauce may be added to raw oysters before dredging them in the dry ingredients to give less flavorful oysters a little help.

This is a quick and easy way to fry oysters. An easy dip in the dry ingredients and straight to the oil is all it takes. For best results, fry no more than 1/2 pint at a time.

Serves 4 to 6

1/2 gallon   peanut or canola oil for frying
1 pint   oysters, drained

Cornmeal Breading

3/4 cup   all-purpose flour
3/4 cup   cornmeal
1/3 cup   cornstarch
3/4 teaspoon   fine sea salt
3/4 teaspoon   white pepper
1/4 teaspoon   freshly ground black pepper

Sift the ingredients together. Reserve.

Preheat the frying oil to 350 degrees.

Place some of the oysters in the breading and toss them to coat well. Allow them to rest in the breading for 1 minute or so. Remove them from the breading and shake off the excess. Fry the oysters until they are crispy and light golden brown in color, about 2 minutes. Remove and place on paper towels. Season more with salt if desired. Serve with Jalapeño and Lime Aïoli.

Jalapeño and Lime Aïoli

Makes ½ cup

1 tablespoon	roughly chopped jalapeño pepper, seeds and all
½ cup	mayonnaise
1 tablespoon	fresh lime juice
1 tablespoon	chopped fresh parsley
¼ teaspoon	fine sea salt

Place all of the ingredients in a food processor with the steel blade. Process until the jalapeño and the parsley are puréed. Refrigerate.

Down South Egg Rolls

with Red Pepper Sauce, Spicy Mustard, and Peach Chutney

Assembling the evening's specials one day, I knew that I wanted to use chicken, tasso, and collards in some item. As the sous chef arrived for work, I tossed it out for ideas. He quickly suggested an egg roll. After a few adjustments and a lot of egg rolls, it became one of our most popular starters and has been a favorite for all these years.

Makes 8 egg rolls

2 tablespoons	light olive oil
2 cups	julienned yellow onions
1 tablespoon plus 1 teaspoon	minced garlic
1 pound	boneless, skinless chicken breasts, fat removed and cut into thin strips
1 cup	small strips tasso
2 cups	packed cooked, chopped collard greens, well drained (see p. 102)
8	egg roll wrappers
2 tablespoons	cornstarch for sealing
2 teaspoons	cold water
1 cup	cornstarch for dusting
12 cups	peanut oil or canola oil for frying

Heat the olive oil in a large heavy-bottomed frying pan over medium-high heat. Add the onions, garlic, chicken, and tasso. Sauté, stirring, for 5 minutes, or until the chicken is fully cooked. Squeeze all of the juice from the collard greens and add them to the frying pan. Cook for 1 to 2 minutes to heat the collards and meld all the flavors. Spread the mixture out onto a pan and let cool. Then squeeze out as much moisture as you can. The drier, the better.

Lay the egg roll wrappers on a clean, dry surface dusted lightly with cornstarch, setting them up in a diamond pattern. Portion $3/4$ cup of the filling on the center of each wrapper. Place the cornstarch in a small bowl and slowly add the cold water, stirring until you have a smooth paste that is free of lumps. Lightly brush the edges of each egg roll wrapper with the mixture of cornstarch and water. Fold the bottom quarter of the diamond up toward the top. Fold the two sides inward to form an envelope. Bring the top corner over toward you. Gently press the edges to seal the rolls. Lightly dust the egg rolls with cornstarch to keep them dry.

Put the peanut or canola oil in a deep fryer or deep frying pan. If you are using something smaller, use only enough oil to fill it about three-quarters of the way up the sides. Gradually heat the oil to 340 degrees by starting to heat it over medium heat and slowly increasing the heat to medium-high. (Never put oil in any frying container and turn the heat on high! Increase heat gradually.)

Put only 4 egg rolls in the hot oil at one time. Too many egg rolls in the oil will bring down the temperature of the oil. Try to keep the temperature as close to 340 degrees as possible.

Fry the egg rolls, turning frequently, until they all are golden brown and crispy. Initially, you should try to keep the egg rolls submerged. As they brown, they will float to the top. If the oil is too hot, the egg roll skins will brown before the egg roll becomes warm throughout. Remove the egg rolls from the oil and place on paper towels to absorb any excess oil. Serve at once with Red Pepper Sauce, Spicy Mustard, and Peach Chutney. For 8 egg rolls you will need $1^1/2$ cups of each accompaniment.

Helpful Hint: Egg roll wrappers: These pasta-like sheets become crispy and bubbly when fried. They can be found in the refrigerated section of most grocery stores.

Red Pepper Sauce

Along with the Spicy Mustard and Peach Chutney, this makes the perfect accompaniment for our Down South Egg Rolls and our Pepper-Seared Sea Scallops with Pimiento Cheese Grits.

Makes 3½ cups

2 tablespoons plus 1 teaspoon	light olive oil
½ cup	roughly chopped yellow onion
1 teaspoon	roughly chopped garlic
¼ cup	all-purpose flour
2½ cups	Chicken Broth (see p. 17)
1½ cups	red pepper flesh from 3 large roasted red peppers (see p. 36), chopped, or 3 (4-ounce) jars pimientos, drained and chopped
¼ cup	chopped fresh basil
	Salt to taste
Pinch	of cayenne pepper

Heat the olive oil in a heavy-bottomed saucepan over medium heat. Add the onion and garlic and sauté for 1 minute. Reduce the heat and make a roux by adding the flour and stirring until well combined. Continue to cook over low heat for 2 minutes, stirring constantly. Do not let the onions or flour color. Turn up the heat to medium and, stirring vigorously, add 1¼ cups chicken broth. Continue stirring vigorously until the broth thickens and is smooth. Gradually add the remaining chicken broth, red pepper strips or pimiento, and basil, stirring constantly until the broth thickens into a sauce.

Bring the sauce to a low boil, then simmer over medium heat for 10 minutes to cook out the starchy flavor of the flour. Skim off any skin that may come to the top and discard. Remove the sauce from the stove and let it cool, stirring occasionally, for 10 minutes. Purée the mixture in a food processor or blender until smooth. Season to taste with salt and cayenne pepper. Use at once or place in a storage container, let cool to room temperature, cover, and refrigerate. Red Pepper Sauce will keep for a week in the refrigerator.

Spicy Mustard

Makes 1½ cups

1 tablespoon	light olive oil
½ cup	roughly chopped yellow onion
½ cup	roughly chopped unpeeled gingerroot
1 teaspoon	chopped garlic
1	chopped jalapeño pepper
½	lemon
½	orange
½ cup	soy sauce
1 cup	Colmans dry mustard
6 ounces	cold water

Heat the olive oil in a heavy-bottomed saucepan over medium heat to just below the smoking point. Add the onion, ginger, garlic, and jalapeño. Sauté for 2 minutes. Cut the lemon and orange into quarters and squeeze the juice over the vegetables. Rough chop the rinds and add them. Add the soy sauce. Cook for 5 minutes over medium heat. Strain and press out the juices. Discard the solids and reserve the juice.

While this is cooking, place the dry mustard in a small mixing bowl and slowly add the water, stirring until you have a smooth paste that is free of lumps. Let this mixture sit for 10 minutes, then stir into the soy sauce mixture. Use at once or cool at room temperature, place in a storage container, cover, and refrigerate. Spicy Mustard will keep for 2 to 3 weeks in the refrigerator.

Peach Chutney

Makes 1$\frac{1}{2}$ cups

2 cups	peeled fresh or frozen peaches
$\frac{1}{2}$ cup	minced yellow onion
1 tablespoon plus 1 teaspoon	peeled and finely minced ginger
$\frac{1}{2}$ cup	finely diced red bell pepper
$\frac{1}{2}$ cup	light brown sugar
$\frac{1}{2}$ cup	granulated sugar
2 tablespoons	cider vinegar

Place all of the ingredients in a heavy-bottomed saucepan over medium heat and stir well to combine. Reduce the heat and cook slowly over low heat for 25 to 30 minutes, stirring occasionally until chutney begins to thicken slightly and is syrupy. Use at once or place the mixture in a storage container, let cool to room temperature, cover, and refrigerate. Peach Chutney will keep for 2 to 3 weeks in the refrigerator.

Helpful Hint: If using fresh peaches, select fairly firm ones that are just beginning to ripen and display a peach flavor. Fully ripened fruit will break down in the cooking process.

Bowtie Pasta

with Applewood-Smoked Bacon, Sun-Dried Tomatoes, Blue Cheese, and Cracked Pepper Cream Sauce

This was one of the most popular dishes on our original menu. The applewood-smoked bacon brings this dish to a whole new level. I use the Nueske's brand. You may oil the noodles after you cook them if you prefer. I find that the sauce will stick to them better if they are not oiled.

Serves 6

2 tablespoons	fine sea salt
10 ounces	bowtie pasta
1 tablespoon	light olive oil
1/4 cup	minced onion
1 teaspoon	minced garlic
1/2 cup	chopped applewood-smoked bacon
1/3 cup	sun-dried tomatoes
1 3/4 cups	heavy cream
3	ounces blue cheese
1 teaspoon	freshly ground black pepper
3 tablespoons	chopped fresh parsley

Bring 1 gallon of water to a boil in a large pot, add the salt, and cook the bowtie pasta for 8 minutes. Drain and place in an ice bath until cool. Remove and drain again.

Heat the oil in a large saucepan and sauté the onion without browning it for 2 to 3 minutes, or until translucent. Add the garlic and cook for 1 minute. Add the bacon, sun-dried tomatoes, cream, 2/3 of the blue cheese, the pepper, and 2 tablespoons of the parsley. Allow the sauce to cook slowly over medium-low heat until it reduces and thickens slightly. Add the cooked bowtie pasta and toss until heated throughout. Divide between six serving dishes. Garnish with the remaining parsley and crumbles of the remaining blue cheese.

Grilled Mahi-Mahi Soft Tacos

with Black Beans and Rice, Guacamole, and Tomato Salsa

It's true: a local favorite game fish with a Hawaiian name is so good that they named it twice! To make a family-style meal, have all the accompaniments ready before you grill the mahi-mahi.

Serves 6 to 8, family-style

3 pounds	fresh mahi-mahi fillets, darker flesh removed
2 tablespoons	Magnolias' Everyday Spicy Dry Rub (see p. 20)
2 tablespoons	light olive oil
1 recipe	Black Beans (see p. 107)
1 recipe	Carolina Aromatic Rice (see p. 95)
12	(8-inch) flour tortillas
	Guacamole
	Tomato Salsa
2 cups	grated cheddar cheese
2 1/2 cups	shredded lettuce
1 1/2 cups	chopped tomato
1 cup	sliced scallions
1 cup	sour cream
1/3 cup	pickled jalapeños
1	lime, cut into wedges

Fire your grill and preheat an oven to 200 degrees.

Trim the mahi-mahi fillets into manageable-size pieces for grilling. Season with the dry rub and drizzle with the olive oil. Allow to marinate while the grill is heating.

Combine the Black Beans and Carolina Aromatic Rice and heat. Wrap the tortillas loosely in foil and heat them in the 200-degree oven for 6 to 8 minutes.

Place the fillets skin-side up and flesh-side down on the heated grill. Sear them for 2 to 3 minutes, or until lightly charred or golden. This gives the fish great flavor. When the flesh-side has nice color, turn the fish over and continue to cook through. Place on a serving platter, and allow to rest for a few minutes. Break the fillets into pieces with tongs or a knife.

Place the warmed flour tortillas on a platter. Serve with the fillets. Serve guacamole, tomato salsa and remaining ingredients buffet-style in individual bowls and let everyone make their own choices. Or, sprinkle the tacos with cheese, add 1/4 cup mahi-mahi, and a combination of the toppings listed above. Serve the black beans and rice as a side dish.

Guacamole

Makes 1 cup

2	ripe avocados (Hass variety preferred)
2 tablespoons	fresh lime juice
1 tablespoon	finely chopped cilantro leaves
1/2 teaspoon	cumin
1/2 teaspoon	fine sea salt

Place the ripe avocado flesh into a bowl and mash. Add the lime juice, cilantro, cumin, and salt. Mix well. If holding for a period of time, cover the surface of the guacamole directly with plastic wrap to eliminate oxidizing, which browns the avocado.

Tomato Salsa

For the best salsa, always buy the freshest tomatoes that are available. For mild salsa, remove the jalapeño pepper's ribs and seeds; for spicy salsa, leave them.

Makes 4 cups

2	fresh, ripe summer tomatoes
1/2 cup	finely diced sweet onion
2 teaspoons	minced garlic
1 teaspoon	minced jalapeño pepper
2 tablespoons	minced fresh Italian parsley
1/4 cup	thinly sliced scallions
3 tablespoons	extra-virgin olive oil
1 tablespoon	red wine vinegar
1/2 teaspoon	salt
1/2 teaspoon	freshly ground black pepper

Core and then slice off the top and the bottom of each tomato. Cut them in half and lightly squeeze out some of the juice. Dice the tomatoes into a small dice and toss them with the other ingredients. Refrigerate the salsa until ready to use.

Soups
and
Salads

Magnolias

Blue Crab Bisque

This is our version of she-crab soup. It has a delicately balanced flavor of cream, sherry, crab, crab roe, and mace. It must have the roe, as it is what gives this lowcountry favorite its unique flavor.

Makes 12 (8-ounce) servings

12 tablespoons	butter
1½ cups	celery, pulsed to a fine mince in a food processor with steel blade
1½ cups	onion, pulsed to a fine mince in a food processor with steel blade
1 cup	all-purpose flour
4 cups	clam juice, room temperature
4 cups	milk, room temperature
1 tablespoon	fresh lemon juice
2	bay leaves
1 tablespoon	Worcestershire sauce
6 ounces	sherry
¼ teaspoon	mace
½ cup	heavy cream
¾ cup	blue crab roe, picked over to remove cartilage, shell, or other matter
1 pound	lump crabmeat, gently picked over for shell and drained of any liquid
2 teaspoons	fine sea salt
Pinch	white pepper
4 tablespoons	sliced chives

Heat the butter in a heavy-bottomed saucepan over medium heat without browning. Add the celery and onions and cook for 1 to 2 minutes, or until the onion is translucent. Sprinkle in the flour while stirring to make a roux. Cook over low heat for 2 to 3 minutes to cook out some of the starchy flavor of the flour.

Whisk the clam juice into the warm roux. Increase the heat to medium-high. Whisk vigorously as the clam juice thickens and is smooth. Whisk in the milk, and allow the mixture to re-thicken, whisking until smooth again. Simmer 1 to 2 minutes. Add the lemon juice, bay leaves, Worcestershire, sherry, mace, cream, crab roe, and crabmeat. Let simmer lightly for 10 to 15 minutes, stirring occasionally. Remove the bay leaves and discard. Add the salt and white pepper. Ladle the bisque into warmed bowls and garnish with chives and a few additional drops of sherry, if desired.

Creamy Tomato Bisque

with Lump Crabmeat and Chiffonade of Fresh Basil

Inspired by my grandparents with their garden-fresh tomatoes, this soup has been everyone's favorite. The fresh tomatoes, fresh basil, and sweet crabmeat make a winning combination.

Makes 8 (10-ounce) servings

4 tablespoons	butter
1/2 cup	chopped yellow onion
1 teaspoon	chopped garlic
1/2 cup	all-purpose flour
3 cups	chicken broth
1	chicken bouillon cube
4 cups	homemade tomato sauce or 2 (14 1/2-ounce) cans tomato sauce
2 cups	tomato juice
3	large peeled fresh vine ripened tomatoes, chopped, or 1 (14 1/2-ounce) can crushed tomatoes with juice
3/4 cup	thinly sliced fresh basil, loosely packed
1 cup	heavy cream
1/2	teaspoon salt
Dash	white pepper
1/2 pound	fresh lump crabmeat, gently picked over for shell

Heat the butter in a heavy-bottomed stockpot over low heat without browning it. Add the onion and garlic. Sauté for 2 to 3 minutes, stirring until the onion is translucent. Reduce the heat and make a roux by adding the flour and stirring until well combined. Continue to cook over low heat for 5 minutes stirring constantly. Increase the heat to medium and add 1 1/2 cups of the chicken broth, whisking vigorously. Gradually add the remaining chicken broth and the bouillon cube, whisking constantly until the broth thickens again. Reduce the heat to low and simmer for 5 minutes.

Add the tomato sauce, tomato juice, chopped tomatoes, and 1/2 cup sliced basil. Simmer for 10 minutes. Skim off any foam on the surface and discard. Add the cream. Bring to a simmer and skim again if necessary. Taste and add the salt and white pepper. Place 1 cup of the hot soup in each of eight bowls. Garnish by sprinkling the crabmeat and the remaining basil over the soup. Serve immediately.

Potato, Leek, and Roasted Garlic Soup

with Creek Shrimp and Tomato Chive Salsa

The easiest way to clean the sand out of leeks is to wash them after they are cut. Immerse them in a deep sink or bowl of cold water. Agitate the leeks by hand to help release the dirt and sand. If the leeks are really dirty, repeat this process. The leeks will float on top of the water, and should be gently removed from the sink or bowl while they are still floating. This assures that there will be no traces of dirt or sand on the leeks, as it will settle on the bottom of the sink or bowl.

Makes 8 (10-ounce) servings

5 tablespoons	unsalted butter
8 cups	roughly cut leeks, washed thoroughly (6 large leeks)
6 cups	peeled and quartered red potatoes
1/3 cup	Roasted Garlic (see p. 25)
4 cups	Chicken Broth (see p. 17)
6 cups	water
2 cups	heavy cream
2 tablespoons	fine sea salt
Pinch	white pepper

In a large heavy-bottomed soup pot, heat the butter without letting it brown. Add the leeks and cook over low heat until they become soft. Add the potatoes, roasted garlic, chicken broth, and water and bring to a boil. Reduce to a simmer and continue to cook the potatoes for 30 to 40 minutes, or until they are very tender. Skim off any foam and discard.

Remove the soup from the heat and allow it to cool slightly. Purée the soup with a handheld blender, food processor, or traditional blender. (It is much easier to do this with a handheld blender. You must let the soup cool longer and be very careful when using a food processor or traditional blender. Only fill them half way and, if you use a blender, leave a little gap in the lid to allow the steam to escape and place a dry kitchen towel over the lid to prevent it from popping off.)

Strain the soup and put it back into a clean soup pot. Bring it up to a simmer over medium heat, removing any foam with a spoon or ladle and discarding it. Add the cream, salt, and white pepper to taste. Place it in an ice bath or cool to room temperature, put in a storage container, cover loosely, and refrigerate until chilled.

Creek Shrimp

1½ pounds   small creek shrimp, peeled, deveined, and split lengthwise

Cook the shrimp in salted water for around 1 minute, or until they turn pink. Immediately chill in an ice bath. Refrigerate.

Tomato Chive Salsa

Makes 2½ cups

2 cups	finely diced fresh tomato without juice or seeds
3 tablespoons	finely sliced fresh chives
2	minced scallions, white part only
3 tablespoons	extra-virgin olive oil
	Salt
	Freshly ground black pepper

Toss the tomatoes, 2 tablespoons of the chives, the scallions, and olive oil together. Add salt and pepper to taste. Let the salsa sit for 20 minutes for the flavors to meld.

To serve, place the soup in chilled shallow bowls. Place the shrimp in the center of the soup and spoon the salsa over the shrimp. Garnish with the remaining chives and serve immediately.

Cajun Clam Chowder

This chowder is a spicier version of the New England clam chowder. You may add a few leaves of fresh cilantro and a couple dashes of hot sauce for an extra bang. The finished chowder isn't designed to be extremely thick; it should be creamy and only thick enough to coat a spoon.

Makes 12 (10-ounce) servings

1/2 cup	chopped smoked bacon
1 cup	diced yellow onion, cut in 1/4-inch dice
1 tablespoon	minced garlic
2 tablespoons	minced jalapeño pepper
1/2 cup	finely chopped tasso
6 tablespoons	olive oil
1 cup	all-purpose flour
3 cups	chopped clams, drained, but juice reserved
3 cups	clam juice, or chicken broth if clam juice is not available
3 cups	chopped baking potatoes, peeled and cut in 1/2-inch dice
2 teaspoons	Magnolias' Blackening Spice (see p. 21)
1 cup	heavy cream
	Salt, white pepper, and cayenne pepper to taste
1/2 cup	chopped chives

In a heavy-bottomed stockpot over medium heat, render the fat from the chopped bacon without browning the bacon. Add the onion, garlic, jalapeño, and tasso. Sauté over medium heat for 2 to 3 minutes, or until the onion is translucent. Add the olive oil. Make a roux by adding the flour gradually and stirring until well combined. Continue to cook over low heat for 5 minutes, stirring very frequently.

Turn the heat up to medium and add the reserved clam juice and the 3 cups of clam juice or chicken broth, one-third at a time, whisking vigorously. With each addition of liquid, it is important to keep whisking constantly until the mixture thickens and is smooth. When all the liquid is added, bring it back to a boil. Add the potatoes and the Blackening Spice. Reduce the heat and simmer over low heat for 30 minutes, or until the potatoes are tender. Stir the potatoes frequently while they are cooking so that they do not settle to the bottom of the pot and scorch. Add the strained clams and cream. Stir to combine and cook over low heat for another 1 to 2 minutes, or until the chowder is heated through. Season to taste with salt, white pepper, and cayenne pepper. Garnish with the fresh chives.

Elwood's Ham Chowder

This chowder has become quite popular over the years. I stumbled upon its main ingredient while trying to figure out what to fix on a rainy winter day. When I came across these Carolina ham trimmings in the grocery store, I knew that they offered a world of opportunity. I made my way back to the produce section and assembled the components that I thought would best complement this newly found ingredient. My father, Elwood, was in town and he helped me put together the first batch. Since its creation, it has been featured by *Martha Stewart Magazine, The Best American Recipes 2003–2004* cookbook, and by Turner South Network on Blue Ribbon. This is a unique dish that melds all of the flavors of the South into chowder like none other. It's much easier to dice up the ham if you freeze it. It's already sliced, so you can just cut it into strips and then into small cubes.

Makes 12 (10-ounce) servings

1 tablespoon	vegetable oil
1 pound	Carolina Ham Trimmings, coarsely ground or minced
3 cups	medium-diced onions
2 tablespoons	sliced garlic
12 cups	stemmed and diced fresh collards
1½ tablespoons	fresh thyme
2 tablespoons	chopped fresh parsley
1 (28-ounce) can	whole tomatoes with juice
7 cups	Chicken Broth (see p. 17)
1 pint	beef stock, homemade or good quality store-bought
6 cups	diced red potatoes, cut in ¼-inch dice
1½ teaspoons	freshly ground black pepper
1½ teaspoons	Tabasco
	Salt

Heat the vegetable oil in a heavy pot. Add the ham and render the fat from the ham by cooking it slowly over medium heat, stirring frequently to keep it from browning. Add the onions and garlic. Continue to cook over low heat, stirring occasionally, until the onions and garlic are soft. A little more oil may be needed if the ham doesn't have enough fat. Slowly add the collards and allow them to wilt. This should be done in two batches, as the collards are very bulky raw, but wilt down like any greens. Add the herbs, tomatoes with juice, chicken broth, beef stock, and red potatoes. Slowly bring the mixture up to a simmer and continue to cook 20 to 30 minutes, or until the potatoes are cooked through. Skim the chowder of any foam or oil that may appear during the cooking process. Add the black pepper and Tabasco. Season to taste with salt and more Tabasco if desired.

Black Bean Chili

with Scallion-and-Cilantro Sour Cream

I made this award-winning chili for the 1991 South Carolina Chili Cook-off. It was featured on Magnolias' first menu. Its unique ginger flavor and "beanie" broth with chunks of pork make it a hearty and satisfying main course.

Makes 16 (8-ounce) portions

Black Beans

4 cups	dried black beans, or 4 (15-ounce cans), drained but not rinsed
16 cups	Chicken Broth (see p. 17)

Measure the dried black beans and pour them onto a cookie sheet. Pick through them to look for small pebbles and discolored beans. Put the beans in a colander and rinse.

Using a heavy-bottomed saucepan, combine the beans and chicken broth and bring to a boil. Reduce to a simmer and cook for about 2 hours, or until the beans are very soft but before their skins start to break. Add additional water if needed, a cup at a time. Strain the beans over a large pot or bowl to catch the juice to use in the chili.

Pork

5 pound	pork shoulder or Boston butt, trimmed of all fat and sinew, or well trimmed and coarsely round by the butcher
1 tablespoon	olive oil
1 tablespoon	minced garlic
2 tablespoons	freshly ground black pepper

Preheat an oven to 450 degrees.

Once the beans are cooking, cut the pork shoulder into 1/2-inch dice or smaller, removing as much fat and sinew as possible, or have a butcher coarsely grind it. Lightly toss the pork with the olive oil, garlic, and black pepper. Spread the pork out onto two baking sheets with raised edges to hold the juices. Roast the pork for approximately 1 hour, or until the meat is nicely browned, but not black. Remove the pork, but save all of the juices and brown bits on the baking sheets. When the pork is cool, break it into the diced pieces again and reserve.

Chili

¼ cup	olive oil
4 cups	roughly chopped yellow onions
4 tablespoons	minced garlic
5 tablespoons	peeled and minced fresh ginger
2 tablespoons	minced jalapeño pepper
5 cups	Chicken Broth (see p. 17)
2	smoked pork neck bones
6 ounces	tomato paste
2 teaspoons	freshly ground black pepper
1 tablespoon	cumin
2 tablespoons	chopped cilantro

Heat the olive oil in a heavy-bottomed pot over medium heat. Add the onion, garlic, 4 tablespoons ginger, and the jalapeño and sauté, stirring, for 2 to 3 minutes, until the onions are translucent. Add the browned pork, chicken broth, neck bones, tomato paste, the reserved juices from the pork, and the juices from the cooked black beans. Let the pork and vegetables simmer over low heat for 40 minutes, or until the pork is quite tender, but not stringy. Add the cooked black beans, 1 teaspoon black pepper, and the cumin. Cook uncovered for 10 to 15 minutes over low heat until the flavors join and the consistency of chili is reached. Remove the neck bones and discard.

Five minutes before you are ready to serve the chili, add the cilantro, the remaining tablespoon of ginger, and the remaining teaspoon of black pepper and continue to cook over low heat to preserve these fresh flavors.

Pour the chili into warm soup bowls and add a dollop of the Scallion and Cilantro Sour Cream on top of each bowl.

Scallion-and-Cilantro Sour Cream

1 cup	sour cream
2 tablespoons	minced scallions
1 tablespoon	minced red bell pepper
½ teaspoon	minced garlic
1 tablespoon	chopped cilantro
½ teaspoon	cumin
½ teaspoon	salt
¼ teaspoon	freshly ground black pepper

Combine the sour cream, scallions, red bell pepper, garlic, cilantro, cumin, salt, and pepper. Mix well. Serve at once or place in a covered storage container and refrigerate.

Shrimp and Rice Salad

with Lemon, Garlic, and Dill Vinaigrette

A great refreshing chilled summer salad. The lemon, garlic, and dill vinaigrette adds a great flavor enhancement to the rice, and the celery and corn give it a sweet flavor and a crunchy texture.

Serves 10 to 12

Rice

2 cups	Carolina Plantation Aromatic Rice (about 1 pound)
3 1/4 cups	water

Rinse the rice with cold water until the water is clear. Place the rice and the water in a deep, heavy-bottomed pot and cover with a lid. Place the pot over medium-low heat and allow it to slowly come to a boil. Reduce the heat and cook the rice slowly for 12 to 15 minutes. It's best not to peek and allow the steam to escape. When the rice has finished cooking, steam holes should be present at the surface of the rice and all of the water should have been absorbed by the rice.

Remove the pot from the heat and fluff the rice with a fork. Spread it out on a large pan or bowl to cool, fluffing frequently to release the steam. Cool to room temperature and reserve.

Salad

1 pound	large shrimp, peeled, deveined, split lengthwise, cooked, and chilled
1 1/2 cups	sweet corn kernels, cooked on the cob, cooled, and cut off (about 2 ears of corn)
1 cup	finely diced celery
1 cup	thinly sliced scallions, using entire scallion
	Lemon, Garlic, and Dill Vinaigrette

Mix together the rice, shrimp, corn, celery, scallions, and herbs. Add 1½ cups of the vinaigrette and toss. Season with salt and white pepper to taste. Chill at least 2 hours or overnight. Add the remaining vinaigrette as needed to refresh the salad just before serving.

Place a small amount in the center of a plate and garnish with a drizzle of the vinaigrette, a sprig of fresh dill and a lemon wedge. You may also serve this salad family style for a picnic or large function.

Lemon, Garlic, and Dill Vinaigrette

Makes 2½ cups

3 tablespoons	spicy Dijon mustard
2 tablespoons	crushed fresh garlic
⅓ cup	fresh lemon juice
¼ cup	rice wine vinegar
1½ cups	light olive oil
⅓ cup	fresh dill sprigs picked from the main stem and cut in medium thin slices
	Fine sea salt
	Ground white pepper

In a mixing bowl, combine the mustard, garlic, lemon juice, and rice wine vinegar and mix well. Slowly whisk in the oil until all is incorporated. Season with salt and white pepper to taste.

Red Potato and Parsley Salad

I prefer to use raw onion in this salad because of my love for it. For a milder flavor, you could sauté the onions, garlic, and parsley in the olive oil, cool, and add as directed.

4 servings

1½ cups	diced red potatoes with skin on, cut in ½-inch dice
1 tablespoon	salt
1 tablespoon	finely minced parsley
1 tablespoon	very finely minced yellow onion
1 tablespoon	very finely minced garlic, mashed to a paste
2 tablespoons	extra-virgin olive oil
	Salt
	Freshly ground black pepper

Place the potatoes, salt, and enough water to cover potatoes in a heavy-bottomed saucepan over medium heat. Bring them to a boil and let simmer for 8 to 10 minutes. The potatoes should be fork tender, and not falling apart.

Put ice cubes in a bowl of cold water and set aside. Drain the potatoes. Rinse with cold water and immerse the potatoes in ice water to stop the cooking. When the potatoes are cold, drain them and place them on paper towels to absorb the excess water.

Combine the parsley, onion, garlic, and olive oil in a medium bowl. Add the potatoes and toss. Add salt and freshly ground black pepper to taste. Serve immediately or refrigerate and serve chilled.

Summer Tomato and Vidalia Onion Salad

This salad is only as good as the quality of the tomato and the mildness of the onion.

Serves 4

2	peak-of-the-season tomatoes
	Vidalia Onion Salad
1 tablespoon	Italian parsley chiffonade
1 teaspoon	coarse sea salt

Gently rinse the tomatoes with cold water and hand dry. Slice very thin (1/8 inch) and arrange in a circle of overlapping slices. Place a little nest of the onion salad in the center. Drizzle with some of the marinade from the Onion Salad and sprinkle with the parsley and sea salt.

Vidalia Onion Salad

Makes 2 cups

2 cups	thinly sliced rings Vidalia onions
2 tablespoons	mayonnaise
3 tablespoons	white vinegar
1 tablespoon	sugar
1/8 teaspoon	fine sea salt
2 tablespoons	extra-virgin olive oil
	Dash white pepper

Place the onion, mayonnaise, vinegar, sugar, salt, olive oil, and pepper in a bowl. Toss together and allow to marinate from 20 minutes to 1 hour in the refrigerator.

Arugula Salad

with Creamy Goat Cheese, Roasted Peppers, and Roasted Garlic Vinaigrette

The roasted garlic gives the salad a great flavor because roasting garlic makes it surprisingly mild. If you are a real garlic lover, you can eat it all by itself as a spread on good bread. If you can't find a creamy goat cheese, you can work some cream into a dry goat cheese to give it a lighter consistency. Otherwise, just crumble the dry goat cheese over the salad. The vinaigrette will make up for some of the moisture. Garnish the salad with lemon slices, if desired.

Serves 6

Roasted Garlic

30	whole peeled garlic cloves
	Water, as needed
2 tablespoons	light olive oil
¹/₄ teaspoon	salt
¹/₄ teaspoon	freshly ground black pepper

Preheat an oven to 475 degrees.

Take the garlic cloves and place them in a small oven-proof skillet or saucepan with the water, oil, salt, and pepper. Add enough water so it is halfway up the sides of the garlic cloves. Bring the mixture to a boil, and place the whole pan in the oven for about 20 minutes. The water will evaporate and the garlic cloves will take on a light golden color and develop a starchy soft texture.

Vinaigrette

Makes 1½ cups

1 tablespoon	Dijon mustard
⅓ cup	cider vinegar
2 tablespoons	fresh lemon juice
1 cup	light olive oil
2 tablespoons	minced shallots
2 tablespoons	sliced chives
½ teaspoon	salt
½ teaspoon	freshly ground black pepper
30	fresh garlic cloves, peeled and roasted

In a medium-sized bowl, mix together the mustard, vinegar, and lemon juice. Slowly pour in the oil in a steady stream, whisking vigorously until all is incorporated. Add the minced shallots, chives, salt, and pepper. Mash 5 of the roasted garlic cloves, chop them to a paste, and add to the vinaigrette. Keep at room temperature until ready to serve.

Arugula Salad

¼ pound	fresh, young arugula leaves, clean and dry
	Salt
	Freshly ground black pepper
½ pound	goat cheese, creamy preferred
1	roasted red bell pepper, cut into strips

To assemble the salad:

Place the arugula in a large bowl and toss lightly with a small amount of the vinaigrette until the leaves are well coated. Season the arugula with a little salt and pepper to taste. Place the arugula in the center of the plates. Place the goat cheese in a piping bag with a star tip and pipe three rosettes of the goat cheese around the arugula, or simply dollop it on. Garnish the salad with the roasted peppers and the remaining roasted garlic cloves. Drizzle with additional vinaigrette if desired.

Iceberg Salad

with Buttermilk, Basil, and Blue Cheese Dressing, Carolina Ham Cracklings, and Grape Tomatoes

I find that this is a very simple salad that everyone loves. The cracklings add a special touch with their cured ham flavor, a contrast to the smoky bacon that is often used.

Serves 6

1 large head iceberg lettuce, picked of its outer leaves, cut into 6 wedges
1 recipe Buttermilk, Basil, and Blue Cheese Dressing (see p. 88)
1 recipe Carolina Ham Cracklings (see p. 22)
½ pint grape tomatoes

Place the wedges of iceberg lettuce on chilled plates and spoon a few table-spoons of the dressing over them. Sprinkle with the cracklings, garnish with the grape tomatoes, and serve immediately.

Warm Sea Scallop Salad
with Lime Dressing over Boston Lettuce

This is a nice warm salad that is quick and easy to make. The lime is balanced with the cream and butter and lightly wilts the Boston lettuce when spooned over.

Serves 4

2 to 3 heads	Boston lettuce, leaves separated, washed, and dried
1 pound	large sea scallops
4 tablespoons	butter
2 tablespoons	minced shallots
3 tablespoons	fresh lime juice
6 tablespoons	heavy cream
1 tablespoon	minced fresh parsley
	Salt
	Freshly ground black pepper

Arrange the lettuce on the plates.

Discard the small muscle attached to the side of the sea scallops. Heat 2 tablespoons of the butter in a sauté pan over medium heat without browning. Add the shallots and the sea scallops and cook for 1 minute. Deglaze the pan with the lime juice and allow it to reduce slightly. Gently turn the scallops over and cook them on the other side for 4 to 5 minutes. They should still be a little translucent in the center. Remove them with a slotted spoon and place on a plate to rest. Add the cream and gently boil to reduce it by half. Turn the heat to low and fold in the remaining butter. Add the parsley and any residual natural juices from the scallops. Season to taste with salt and pepper.

Immediately spoon the scallops over the lettuce leaves, drizzle with the pan dressing, and serve warm.

Classic Caesar Salad

When making a Caesar, I prefer to pull the lettuce from the ribs of the Romaine leaves. This will give you a great leafy salad that is free of rib pieces. It is well worth the effort. And the anchovies, fresh garlic, classic mustard dressing made with fresh lemon juice, and real Parmigiano-Reggiano cheese are a must. Remember that your dish is only as good as your ingredients!

This dressing can be made a few days ahead and always kept on hand. It is an easy way to get the real Caesar flavor without the production during dinner service. It is meant to be thick and somewhat pasty. It is best tossed with the salad when the dressing is close to room temperature.

Serves 4

4	hearts of Romaine, washed, dried, and ribs off

Dressing

Makes ³/₄ cup

8	anchovy fillets
1 tablespoon plus 1 teaspoon	minced garlic
1 tablespoon	Dijon mustard
1	egg yolk (pasteurized)
1¹/₂ teaspoons	fresh lemon juice
6 tablespoons	grated Parmigiano-Reggiano cheese
¹/₄ cup	extra-virgin olive oil
1 tablespoon	water
¹/₂ teaspoon	freshly ground black pepper

With the steel blade attached to your food processor, purée the anchovies and garlic, stopping to scrape down the sides a time or two. Add the mustard, egg yolk, lemon juice, and 4 tablespoons of the cheese. Pulse to combine these ingredients. With the motor running, stream in the extra-virgin olive oil just until incorporated. Place in a small bowl and stir in the water by hand. Season with the black pepper. Refrigerate, if not using immediately.

Croutons

1 tablespoon	garlic, mashed to a paste
2 tablespoons	light olive oil
1/4 teaspoon	fine sea salt
1/4 teaspoon	freshly ground black pepper
3 cups	1/2-inch squares of French bread, crust removed

Preheat an oven to 325 degrees.

Mix the garlic, olive oil, salt, and pepper well to combine. Place the bread squares in a large bowl and toss them evenly with the olive oil mixture. Spread them out evenly on a baking sheet and toast them in the oven for 15 to 20 minutes. The croutons should be golden brown, dried all the way through, and crunchy. Remove from the oven and allow for them to cool completely before using.

To finish the salad:

Place the dressing in the bottom of a wooden bowl and add the Romaine lettuce. Toss until a light consistent coating is on the lettuce. Garnish with croutons and the remaining Parmigiano-Reggiano cheese.

Mixed Greens

with Lemon Herb Vinaigrette

This versatile dressing can act as the base of a number of others, as you will see. Makes 1½ cups, or enough for 8 to 10 salads of mixed lettuce or field greens. I especially like the mixture of red and green oak leaf lettuces, red and green Romaine, and radicchio. You can make excellent variations of the Lemon Herb Vinaigrette, including Lemon Lingonberry Vinaigrette and Tomato Herb Vinaigrette.

Serves 8 to 10

1½ pounds   mixed greens, washed well and dried

Lemon Herb Vinaigrette

2 tablespoons   Dijon mustard
2 tablespoons   cider vinegar
¼ cup   fresh lemon juice
1 cup   light olive oil
2 tablespoons   chopped chives
2 tablespoons   finely julienned then lightly chopped fresh basil
1 teaspoon   minced garlic
¼ teaspoon   freshly ground black pepper

The emulsion for this dressing can be easily done by mixing the mustard, vinegar and lemon juice in a blender. Turn the blender on low speed and slowly stream in the oil, running the blender for only 30 to 40 seconds. The blender method will give you a creamier, fluffier dressing. After blending, place the vinaigrette in a bowl. Stir in the herbs, garlic, and pepper.

If you are making the dressing by hand, put the mustard, vinegar, and lemon juice in a bowl and whisk them together. Add the olive oil very slowly in a steady stream, whisking vigorously until the oil is incorporated. Fold in the herbs, garlic, and pepper.

Use immediately or store the dressing, covered, in a container in the refrigerator. It should easily keep for a day or two before the ingredients separate. If this does occur, you can whisk the dressing back together before putting it on the salads.

Lemon Lingonberry Vinaigrette

Makes 2¹/₂ cups

1 recipe Lemon Herb Vinaigrette
¹/₃ cup lingonberry preserves

Add ¹/₃ cup lingonberry preserves to the Lemon Herb Vinaigrette by folding it in with the herbs. The preserves can be found in specialty shops and on the gourmet shelf of most grocery stores.

Tomato Herb Vinaigrette

Makes 1³/₄ cups

1 recipe Lemon Herb Vinaigrette
1 tomato

Cut the tomato in half and gently squeeze out the juice and seeds. Dice the flesh and add it to the Lemon Herb Vinaigrette by folding it in with the herbs.

Buttermilk, Basil, and Blue Cheese Dressing

Low-fat varieties of mayonnaise, sour cream, and buttermilk may be used with this recipe. In addition to being a good salad dressing, it also works as a dip for fresh vegetables.

Makes 1 3/4 cups or enough for 8 salads of butter lettuce or field greens

1/4 cup	mayonnaise
1/4 cup	sour cream
3/4 cup	buttermilk
1/4 teaspoon	minced garlic
1/4 teaspoon	salt
2 tablespoons	honey
2 tablespoons	cider vinegar
1 tablespoon plus 2 teaspoons	julienned fresh basil
1 cup	Roquefort, Danish blue cheese, or Clemson blue cheese, crumbled but not mashed
	Freshly ground black pepper

Combine the mayonnaise, sour cream, buttermilk, garlic, salt, honey, and vinegar. Whisk lightly to blend until smooth. Fold in the basil and 1/2 cup blue cheese. Season to taste with pepper and more salt, if desired. After the lettuce is tossed in the dressing and put on salad plates, sprinkle the top of the salads with the remaining crumbled blue cheese.

Carolina Peanut Vinaigrette

You may substitute regular vegetable oil for the peanut oil if you increase the
peanut butter by 1 tablespoon. Some peanut oils actually have peanut flavor.
Using one of these will enhance the dressing. I recommend using the dressing
with mixed lettuces, garnished with crushed dry roasted unsalted peanuts
and/or crumbled blue cheese.

Makes 2 cups

3 tablespoons	creamy or low-fat peanut butter
1/2 cup plus 2 tablespoons	cider vinegar
2 tablespoons	light brown sugar
1 1/2 teaspoons	minced garlic
1 1/4 cups	peanut oil
2 teaspoons	minced fresh parsley
2 teaspoons	minced fresh basil
1/2 teaspoon	freshly ground black pepper

Put the peanut butter and cider vinegar in a bowl and whisk them together to
dissolve the peanut butter. Add the sugar and the garlic. Pour the peanut oil
in a slow steady stream, whisking vigorously until the oil is incorporated. Fold
in the herbs and pepper.

Use immediately or store the dressing, covered, in a container in the refrigerator.
It should easily keep for a day or two before the ingredients separate. If this
does occur, you can whisk the dressing back together before using it.

Southern
Sides

Magnolias

Classic Potato Fries

Great fries first need to be blanched in a lower temperature oil to partially cook them, cooled, and then fried at a higher temperature. This can be done hours, even days ahead. To hold for days, spread the blanched fries out on a baking sheet, put the baking sheet in the freezer, and freeze the fries individually. Then put them in freezer bags. They can then be fried in a frozen state as you would commercial fries.

Serves 4

1/2 gallon peanut or canola oil
2 pounds russet potatoes, washed, and cut into 1/4-inch-thick fries
Salt
Freshly ground black pepper

Preheat the oil to 300 degrees.

Rinse the fries in a bowl of cold water, agitate them with your hand gently to release some of the starches, and drain. Repeat this step again. Pat the fries dry with paper towels. Place half of the dried potatoes in a fryer basket and submerge in the heated oil. Blanch them for 3 minutes, gently shaking the basket to agitate them in the oil so that they do not stick together. Lift the basket from the oil and shake off the excess. Place the fries on a baking sheet lined with paper towels and spread them out. Cool them by placing in the freezer while the other half is blanching. Chill the second half of the blanched fries in the freezer.

Increase the heat to 350 degrees. Add blanched fries to the preheated oil and cook them for 2 to 3 minutes, or until golden brown and crispy. Place the fries on paper towels. Season to taste with salt and pepper. Allow to cool slightly before eating.

Butter-Whipped Potatoes

Makes 5 cups

6 cups	large roughly cut peeled russet or boiling potatoes
6 cups	cold water
2 tablespoons plus 1 teaspoon	fine sea salt
1 cup	heavy cream
1/2 cup	half-and-half
6 tablespoons	butter
	White pepper

Put the potatoes, water, and 2 tablespoons salt in a saucepan and bring to a boil over medium-high heat. Lower the heat to a simmer and cook for 18 to 20 minutes, or until the potatoes are tender when pierced with a fork.

Place the cream, half-and-half, and butter in a small saucepan and heat until the butter has melted. Reserve warm.

Drain the liquid off the potatoes and return the pan to the burner. Steam dry the potatoes, stirring constantly. Remove from the heat and put the potatoes thorough a food mill with a fine screen or a potato ricer.

Carefully blend the warm cream mixture into the potatoes. Season with the remaining salt and white pepper to taste. Using a whisk or a mixer with a whisk attachment, whip up the potatoes. Serve immediately.

Parsley Potatoes

Serves 6

20	small new potatoes
1 teaspoon	salt plus more to taste
1 teaspoon	light olive oil
	Freshly ground black pepper
2 tablespoons	finely chopped fresh parsley

With a small knife, cut off the tops and bottoms of the potatoes and pare down the sides, giving them an oval shape.

Place the potatoes in a saucepan with enough water to cover them. Add 1 teaspoon salt. Simmer for 15 minutes, until tender. It is important not to boil the potatoes because boiling them will cook the outside before the inside.

Place ice water in a bowl and set aside. Drain the potatoes. Rinse them in cold water and immerse in the ice water to stop the cooking. Drain and pat dry. Heat the olive oil in a heavy-bottomed skillet over medium heat. Roll the potatoes in the hot oil to lightly brown the outside and warm them through. Add salt and pepper to taste and parsley to please the eye.

Carolina Aromatic Rice

If using a rice steamer, rinse the rice as you usually would and drain well. Use 1 cup of water to 1 cup of rice ratio for steaming the rice. The following is a one-pot method.

Serves 6 to 8

2 cups	Carolina Plantation Aromatic Rice (about 1 pound)
3 cups	water

Rinse the rice with cold water until the water is clear. Place the rice and the water in a deep, heavy-bottomed pot and cover with a lid. Place the pot over medium-low heat and allow it to come to a boil slowly. Reduce the heat and cook the rice slowly for 12 to 15 minutes. It's best not to peek and allow the steam to escape. When the rice has finished cooking, steam holes should be present at the surface of the rice and all of the water should have been absorbed by the rice.

Remove the pot from the heat and fluff the rice with a fork. Serve immediately or spread it out on a large pan to cool, fluffing it frequently to release the steam. Cool to room temperature, place in a container, cover, and refrigerate.

Red Rice

Enhanced with sausage, tasso, and tomato juice, this spicy rice is a great side dish with chicken, pork, and seafood.

Serves 4 to 6

3/4 cup	tomato juice
2 cups	Chicken Broth (see p. 17)
2 tablespoons	tomato paste
1/2 teaspoon	salt
1/4 teaspoon	freshly ground black pepper
Dash	cayenne pepper
6 tablespoons	light olive oil
1/2 cup	chopped yellow onion
1 tablespoon	minced garlic
1/2 cup	chopped celery
1/4 cup	chopped cooked spicy Italian sausage
1/4 cup	finely chopped tasso
2 cups	converted rice (see p. 14)

Preheat an oven to 350 degrees.

Combine the tomato juice, chicken broth, tomato paste, salt, black pepper, and cayenne pepper and reserve. In a heavy-bottomed, oven-proof stockpot, heat the olive oil over medium heat. Add the onion, garlic, celery, sausage, and tasso. Sauté, stirring for 2 to 3 minutes, or until the onions are translucent. Add the rice and stir until the rice is coated with oil. Pour in the tomato juice mixture. Bring to a boil, stirring constantly.

Cover the stockpot and place it in the oven. Bake the rice for about 20 minutes, or until all of the liquid is absorbed and the rice is tender. Uncover the stockpot, fluff the rice with a fork, and season with more salt, black pepper, or cayenne pepper if desired. Serve immediately.

Dirty Rice

This is a hearty rice with lots of depth. The chicken livers give it both flavor and nutritional value. True to its name, it looks dirty, but tastes just fine.

Serves 4 to 6

1 cup	chicken livers
3 tablespoons plus 1 teaspoon	light olive oil
	Salt
	Freshly ground black pepper
1/2 cup	finely chopped yellow onion
1 tablespoon	minced garlic
1/2 cup	cooked and chopped spicy Italian sausage
1/4 cup	chopped tasso
2 cups	converted rice
2 3/4 cups	Chicken Broth (see p. 17)
1/2 cup	chopped scallions
2 to 3 dashes	Tabasco

Preheat an oven to 350 degrees.

Trim any fat and sinew from the livers. Toss the livers, 1 teaspoon olive oil, and a dash of salt and pepper in a bowl. Put the livers on a baking sheet with raised edges and place it on the top rack of the oven. Bake for 20 minutes. Cool the livers, finely chop them, and set aside.

Heat the remaining olive oil in a heavy-bottomed saucepan over medium heat. Add the onion and garlic and sauté them, stirring, for 2 to 3 minutes, or until the onion is translucent. Add the sausage, tasso, and chicken livers and sauté them for 3 minutes. Add the rice and stir until it is coated with the olive oil.

Pour in the chicken broth and bring the mixture to a boil, constantly stirring. Cover the saucepan and place it in the oven. Bake the rice for 20 to 30 minutes, or until all the liquid is absorbed and the rice is tender. Uncover the saucepan, add the scallions, and fluff the rice and onions with a fork. Season with salt, black pepper, and Tabasco to taste. Serve immediately.

Baked Blue Cheese and Macaroni

For those of you who love blue cheese, and macaroni and cheese, as I do, this is a great recipe to have both at once. It makes for an excellent side dish.

Serves 8 to 10, family-style

1 gallon	water
2 tablespoons	salt
16 ounces	macaroni
3 tablespoons	butter
3 tablespoons	all-purpose flour
3 cups	half-and-half, room temperature
1 pound	grated Monterey jack cheese
1 cup	milk
1 teaspoon	fine sea salt
1/2 teaspoon	freshly ground black pepper
1/4 teaspoon	cayenne pepper
6 ounces	blue cheese, crumbled

Bring the water to a boil in a large stockpot. Add the salt just before the macaroni and cook the macaroni for 12 minutes, or until cooked but still firm. Remember, the noodles are going to cook again. Strain and rinse in cold water with a few ice cubes until cooled. Drain and cover loosely. I do not recommend oiling the macaroni noodles.

Preheat an oven to 400 degrees.

Melt the butter in a heavy-bottomed saucepan. Whisk in the flour. Cook over low heat for 1 to 2 minutes. Add 1/2 of the half-and-half and whisk vigorously as it thickens to a smooth paste. Use a spatula to release the mixture that may be stuck in the corners of the pan. Whisk again until smooth and thickened. Add the remaining half-and-half and whisk constantly, slowly bringing the sauce up to a simmer. Cook for 1 to 2 minutes to cook out some of the starchy flavor of the flour.

Add ¾ of the Monterey jack cheese to the thickened half-and-half. When the cheese is melted, add the milk, salt, black pepper, and cayenne pepper. Stir in 5 ounces of the blue cheese and allow it to melt slightly. Place the macaroni in a large bowl and pour the cheese sauce over it. Stir well to coat the macaroni evenly. Pour it into a 9 x 13-inch casserole dish and sprinkle the remaining Monterey jack cheese over the top. Place the baking dish in the upper part of the oven. Allow the macaroni and cheese to bake for 15 minutes. Sprinkle the remaining blue cheese on top. Return to the oven and bake for 15 minutes more, or until the top is golden brown and bubbly. Remove from the oven and allow the macaroni and cheese to rest 5 minutes before serving.

Baked Macaroni and Cheddar Cheese

Serves 8 to 10, family-style

1 gallon	water
2 tablespoons	salt
16 ounces	macaroni
3 tablespoons	butter
3 tablespoons	all-purpose flour
3 cups	half-and-half, room temperature
1 pound	mild yellow cheddar cheese, grated
1 cup	milk
1 teaspoon	fine sea salt
1/2 teaspoon	freshly ground black pepper
1/4 teaspoon	cayenne pepper

Bring the water to a boil in a large stockpot. Add the salt just before the macaroni and cook the macaroni for 12 minutes, or until cooked but still firm. Remember, the noodles are going to cook again. Strain and rinse in cold water with a few ice cubes until cooled. Drain and cover loosely. I do not recommend oiling the macaroni noodles.

Preheat an oven to 400 degrees.

Melt the butter in a heavy-bottomed saucepan. Whisk in the flour. Cook over low heat for 1 to 2 minutes. Add half the half-and-half and whisk vigorously as it thickens to a smooth paste. Use a spatula to release the mixture that may be stuck in the corners of the pan. Whisk again until smooth and thickened. Add the remaining half-and-half and whisk constantly, slowly bringing the sauce up to a simmer. Cook for 1 to 2 minutes to cook out some of the starchy flavor of the flour.

Add 3/4 of the cheese to the thickened half-and-half. When the cheese is melted, add the milk, salt, black pepper, and cayenne pepper. Place the macaroni in a large bowl and pour the cheese sauce over it. Stir well to coat the macaroni evenly. Pour it into a 9 x 13-inch casserole dish and sprinkle the remaining cheddar cheese over the top. Place the baking dish in the upper part of the oven. Allow the macaroni and cheese to bake for 30 minutes, or until the top is golden brown and bubbly. Remove from the oven and allow the macaroni and cheese to rest 5 minutes before serving.

Creamed Corn

This wonderful side dish is a true way to make creamed corn. The goal is to have the natural creaminess of the milk thickened with the starches of the fresh corn kernels. The cream and butter are optional.

Up to 2 tablespoons of sugar may be added in this dish. It really depends on the natural sweetness of the corn you are using and how sweet you like your creamed corn.

Makes 3 cups

5 ears	fresh yellow corn, cleaned of silk
1 3/4 cups	milk
2 tablespoons	cornstarch
2 tablespoons	sugar (optional)
	Salt
	Dash of white pepper
2 tablespoons	heavy cream (optional)
2 tablespoons	butter (optional)

Cut the kernels from the cob. Pulse 2/3 of the kernels in a food processor. Put in a saucepan. Add the whole kernels, milk, cornstarch, and as much sugar as desired. Bring slowly to a boil, stirring constantly, and cook over medium heat for 10 to 15 minutes. Season to taste with salt and white pepper. You may also add the cream and butter to make it more decadent.

Magnolias' Collard Greens

I had never had collard greens until my mother-in-law introduced me to this New Year's Day tradition. I found that cooking them long and slow in chicken broth made them better flavored and silkier in texture. The smoked ham hock or neck bones add a subtle smoky flavor and the acidity of the vinegar and Tabasco gives them a nice tart, yet spicy, flavor.

Serves 4

2 tablespoons	light olive oil
1 cup	diced yellow onion, cut in ¼-inch dice
1 tablespoon	minced garlic
1	smoked ham hock or 2 smoked pork neck bones
3 tablespoons	cider vinegar
12 cups	washed, stemmed, and roughly chopped collard greens (2 large or 3 small bunches)
9 cups	Chicken Broth (see p. 17)
2 teaspoons	Tabasco, or to taste
	Salt
	Freshly ground black pepper

Heat the olive oil in a large heavy-bottomed stockpot over medium heat. Add the onion and garlic and sauté for 2 to 3 minutes, stirring, or until the onion is translucent. Add the ham hock or neck bones and vinegar. Gradually add the collard greens. Cook the greens over medium heat, stirring occasionally, until wilted. As they wilt down, there will be enough room to get them all into the pot. Add the chicken broth and 1 teaspoon Tabasco. Bring to a boil and simmer for 1 hour and 45 minutes to 2 hours, adding more water if necessary, 1 cup at a time, until the greens have a good flavor and are silky in texture. Add the remaining Tabasco and season with salt and pepper to taste.

Lady Peas, White Hall Peas, Black-Eyed Peas, Zipper Peas, and Butter Beans

All of these fresh peas and beans cook from 30 to 35 minutes. If you cook them another 10 minutes and mash some of them with the back of a spoon, the released starch will give them a natural creaminess. A small addition of water may be needed for this step.

Serves 4

3 cups	fresh beans or peas (1 pound)
2 1/2 cups	water
	Smoked pork neck bone or piece of smoked bacon, if desired
3/4 teaspoon	salt
Dash	white pepper
2 tablespoons	butter

Rinse the peas or beans under cold water and remove any foreign particles. Put them in a saucepan and add the water. Add the smoked product, if desired. Cook over medium heat, removing the foam that will appear as they begin to cook and discarding it. Season with the salt, white pepper, and butter.

Slow-Cooked Okra and Tomatoes

The fresher the okra, the better. Look for those that are a vibrant green. I prefer those that are no longer than 2½ inches in length. Leaving the caps on the okra helps to prevent a viscous quality from developing as they cook. The tomato is a natural partner for this Southern vegetable. Its acidity cuts through the textures and tastes that may turn people away from okra altogether.

Serves 8 to 10 okra lovers

4 cups	fresh whole okra (about 1 pound)
3 tablespoons	light olive oil
2 tablespoons	sliced garlic
1½ cups	peeled, seeded, and diced fresh tomatoes
½ cup	tomato juice
⅛ teaspoon	freshly ground black pepper
¼ teaspoon	fine sea salt

Just barely trim the stem end off of the okra and leave the caps on. You don't want to open it through to the seeds. Rinse the okra and pat dry.

Heat the olive oil in a broad, heavy-bottomed pan over medium heat. Add the okra and cook it, stirring occasionally, for 5 minutes so that the okra cooks slow and evenly. Add the garlic and cook for another 5 minutes. Add the tomatoes, tomato juice, pepper, and salt. Cook for 6 minutes, or until the okra is tender and the tomato juices have reduced.

South Carolina Hoppin' John

I don't think that you can get any closer to the real thing for this Southern New Years good luck tradition. We use rice and the cow peas that are grown in Darlington County, South Carolina.

Serves 10 to 12 (Makes 3 quarts)

2 cups	Carolina Plantation dried cowpeas
9 1/2 cups	water
2 ounces	Carolina Ham Trimmings (see p. 13), a smoked pork neck bone, or a ham hock, if desired
1 1/2 cups	Carolina Plantation Aromatic Rice (see p. 14)
2 teaspoons	fine sea salt
1/2 teaspoon	ground white pepper

Pour the peas on a baking sheet with raised sides. Pick over them to check for small pebbles and stems and remove them. Put the peas in a colander and rinse them well with cold water. Place in a stockpot and add 8 cups of the water. Skim off any floating peas. Add the pork, if desired. (I do not put salt in the water at the beginning of this process as it hardens the peas and lengthens the cooking time.)

Cook the peas over medium heat for 1 hour. Add the remaining water and bring back to a boil. Rinse the rice 2 or 3 times in cold water until the water is clear. Stir the rice into the peas. There must be a least 2 1/4 cups of liquid in the peas for the rice to cook. Reduce the heat to low and cover. Continue to cook for another 10 to 12 minutes over low heat without lifting the lid.

When most of the liquid is absorbed and the rice is cooked, fluff the peas and rice, and add the salt and white pepper. Add a little water if necessary. Serve immediately.

Black Beans and
Carolina Aromatic Rice

Serve the beans with steamed Carolina Aromatic Rice as a side dish or alone, topped with chopped onions and sour cream. For a mild version, remove the ribs and seeds from the jalapeño before you mince it. If you like it spicy, leave them attached.

Serves 6 to 8

1 pound	dried black beans
10 cups	water
2 cups	diced yellow onion
2 tablespoons	minced jalapeño pepper
1 tablespoon	minced garlic
1 teaspoon	cumin
1 teaspoon	freshly ground black pepper
Pinch	cayenne pepper
1/2 pound	Carolina Ham Trimmings (optional) (see p. 13)
	Salt
1 recipe	Carolina Aromatic Rice (see p. 95)

Pour the black beans onto a baking sheet with raised edges. Pick over them to check for small pebbles and discolored beans and remove them. Put the beans in a colander and rinse them well with cold water. Place in a stockpot and cover with the 10 cups water. Add the diced vegetables, cumin, black pepper, and cayenne pepper. Add the ham trimmings if desired. (I do not put salt in the water at the beginning of this process, as it hardens the beans and lengthens the cooking time.) Bring the beans to a boil, then reduce the heat to attain a low simmer. Cook the beans for 2 1/2 to 3 hours. An extra cup or two of water may be needed if the beans have cooked too fast. After the beans have softened and a "beanie" broth is obtained, check the seasoning and add salt as needed. If no ham was used, more salt may be required. Season to taste with more black pepper. Combine with rice or serve side by side.

Grits
and
Gravies

Magnolias

Skillet-Seared Yellow Grits Cakes

The trick to this dish is to get a good golden crust when pan-frying, while keeping the inside creamy. The Tasso Gravy and Yellow Corn Relish finish the dish off perfectly.

Makes 8 servings

4 cups	water
1 1/4 cups	coarse stone-ground yellow grits
1/2 cup	heavy cream
	Salt
	White pepper
	Coarsely ground cornmeal
3/4 cup	light olive oil
	Tasso Gravy (see p. 114)
1 tablespoon	chopped fresh parsley
	Yellow Corn Relish (see p. 18)

Bring the water to a boil in a heavy-bottomed stockpot or large saucepan. Slowly pour in the grits, stirring constantly. Reduce the heat to low and continue to stir so that the grits do not settle to the bottom and scorch. After 8 to 10 minutes, the grits will plump up. Cook the grits over low heat for another 30 to 35 minutes, stirring frequently. The grits should become soft and velvety, but still firm in consistency. Stir in the heavy cream and cook for another 8 to 10 minutes, stirring frequently. Season with salt and white pepper to taste.

Line a 9 x 9 x 2-inch pan with waxed paper or spray the pan with non-stick vegetable spray. Pour in the grits and spread them over the bottom of the pan to make an even thickness of 1 1/4-inch. Let the grits cool in the pan at room temperature, then place the pan into the refrigerator for at least 1 hour to firm the grits.

Preheat an oven to 250 degrees.

When ready to serve the dish, cut the grits into 4 equal squares. Then cut each square corner to corner to make triangles. Remove the triangles from the pan and lightly dust them with cornmeal.

Heat 2 tablespoons of the olive oil in a heavy-bottomed frying pan over medium heat. Pan-fry the grits cakes, 4 at a time, turning once, until a golden crust is obtained on both sides. Add additional olive oil to the pan if it is dry. Placed on a baking sheet lined with paper towels, the grits cakes may be held in the oven until all are pan-fried.

Place 1 warm grits cake on each of 8 warm plates. Spoon the Tasso Gravy over the grits cake and sprinkle the parsley. Serve with fresh Yellow Corn Relish.

Creamy White Grits

with Carolina Country Ham and Red-Eye Gravy

Unfortunately, these grits are not the same when refrigerated and reheated. They must be eaten within hours of preparation to enjoy their natural creamy consistency.

Serves 6

6 cups	water
1 2/3 cups	coarse stone-ground white grits
1/2 cup	heavy cream
1 tablespoon	butter
1/2 tablespoon	salt
Dash	white pepper

Bring the water to a boil in a heavy-bottomed stockpot or large saucepan and slowly pour in the grits, stirring constantly. Reduce the heat to low and continue to stir so that the grits do not settle to the bottom and scorch. After 8

to 10 minutes, the grits will plump up. Cook the grits over low heat for another 30 to 35 minutes, stirring frequently. Add the cream, butter, salt and white pepper within the last 15 minutes. The grits will have a thick natural creamy consistency and become soft and silky. Keep covered and warm until ready to serve. If the grits become too thick, add warm water to adjust the consistency.

Carolina Country Ham and Red-Eye Gravy

¼ cup	light olive oil
1 pound	thin slices country ham
2 cups	black coffee
3 tablespoons	butter

Heat the oil in a large, heavy-bottomed frying pan. Place the ham slices in the pan a couple at a time. Do not overcrowd. Allow the ham to caramelize slightly on one side and then flip over and do the same. Continue until all of the ham slices are cooked. Be careful not to burn the drippings that caramelize on the pan surface. Drain off the excess oil and pour in the coffee a little at a time to deglaze the pan. When all of the coffee is added place over medium heat and reduce by half. Whisk the butter into the gravy, place the ham slices over the creamy grits, drizzle with the red-eye gravy, and serve immediately.

Magnolias' Spicy Shrimp, Sausage, and Tasso Gravy over Creamy White Grits

These grits are not the same if reheated after they are refrigerated. They should be cooked within hours of serving.

Serves 8

Grits

Makes 12 cups

12 cups	water
3 1/4	cups coarse stone-ground white grits
1 cup	heavy cream
2 tablespoons	butter
1 tablespoon	salt
1/4 teaspoon	white pepper

Bring the water to a boil in a heavy-bottomed stockpot or large saucepan. Slowly pour in the grits, stirring constantly. Reduce the heat to low and continue to stir so that the grits do not settle to the bottom and scorch. After 8 to 10 minutes, the grits will plump up. Cook the grits over low heat for 30 to 35 minutes, stirring frequently. Add the cream, butter, salt, and white pepper within the last 15 minutes. The grits will have a thick natural creamy consistency and become soft and silky. Keep covered and warm until ready to serve. If the grits become too thick, add warm water to adjust the consistency.

Tasso Gravy

Makes 3 1/2 cups

4 tablespoons	butter
1/2 cup	sliced tasso, cut in 1-inch strips
1/2 cup	all-purpose flour
4 cups	Chicken Broth (see p. 17)
2 tablespoons	finely chopped fresh parsley
	Salt
	White pepper

(continued on page 116)

Melt the butter in a heavy-bottomed saucepan over low heat. Add the tasso. Sauté for 1 minute, browning slightly. Make a roux by adding the flour and stirring until well combined. Continue to cook over low heat for 5 minutes, stirring frequently, or until the roux develops a nutty aroma. Turn the heat up to medium and gradually add 2 cups of the chicken broth, whisking vigorously. Keep whisking constantly until the broth begins to thicken and is smooth. Gradually add the remaining chicken broth, whisking constantly until the broth thickens into gravy. Reduce the heat and simmer over low heat for 15 minutes to cook out the starchy flavor of the flour. Add the parsley. Simmer for another 5 minutes. Season to taste with salt and white pepper.

Shrimp and Sausage

½ pound	spicy Italian sausage
1 tablespoon	light olive oil
2 pounds	medium or large shrimp, peeled and deveined
1½ cups	Chicken Broth (see p. 17)
1 recipe	Tasso Gravy (see p. 114)
2 tablespoons	finely chopped fresh parsley

Preheat an oven to 400 degrees.

Place the sausage on a baking sheet with raised sides. Place it on the top rack of the oven and bake for 10 to 15 minutes, or until it is firm and its juices run clear. Cool and cut into small bite-size pieces. Reserve.

Heat the olive oil in a heavy-bottomed frying pan over medium heat. Add the cooked sausage and sauté for 2 minutes to brown slightly. Add the shrimp and sauté until they just begin to turn pink, no longer than 1 minute. Add 1 cup of chicken broth to de-glaze the pan. Add the Tasso Gravy and 1 tablespoon of the parsley. Bring the mixture up to a gentle boil and simmer for 1 minute, stirring. Use the remaining chicken broth to thin the gravy, if needed.

Divide the hot grits between 8 warm bowls. Spoon the shrimp and sausage mixture over the grits. Sprinkle them with the remaining tablespoon of parsley and serve immediately.

Shellfish with Lobster Sauce over Creamy White Grits

Serves 8

Lobsters

3 (1 ¼-pound)   live Maine lobsters

Lobsters will yield approximately 28 percent of their overall weight when they are cooked and the meat is removed. These three lobsters will yield close to a pound of succulent meat. By making the stock from the shells, then the sauce from the stock, the wonderful result is this buttery lobster sauce, which is actually the same as a classic lobster bisque.

Bring 3 cups water to boil in a large pot with a tight-fitting lid. Place the lobsters on their backs and pierce through their heads between their legs with the tip of a sturdy, sharp knife. Place the lobsters in the pot, cover and steam for 6 to 7 minutes. Meanwhile, prepare an ice bath. Remove the lobsters and immerse them totally in the ice bath to cool. Reserve the pot and the steaming liquid. When the lobsters are cool enough to handle, remove the claws and tails over the pot in order to catch all of the juices. Reserve the meat, the shells, and the liquid in the pot.

Lightly tap the claws on the side to just crack the shells. Remove the claw meat as much intact as possible. Lay the tails on their sides and tap lightly to crack the shells. Remove the tail meat as much intact as possible. Remove the intestinal tracts along the back of the tail meat and discard. Reserve all of the shells. Place the lobster meat in a bowl and refrigerate.

Lobster Stock

Makes 2 cups

4 tablespoons	light olive oil
¾ cup	chopped onion
¾ cup	chopped celery
½ cup	chopped carrot
2	garlic cloves, smashed

(continued on page 119)

3 sprigs	fresh tarragon
6 leaves	fresh basil
2	bay leaves
4	black peppercorns, crushed
1 teaspoon	fine sea salt
	Reserved lobster shells
1 (6-ounce) can	tomato paste

Reserved liquid from cooking lobsters plus enough water to make 8 cups

Heat the oil in a heavy-bottomed pot. Add the onion, celery, and carrot. Cook over low heat until the vegetables are soft, but not caramelized. Add the garlic, tarragon, basil, bay leaves, peppercorns, and salt. Cook for 1 minute. Add the lobster shells. Crush the bodies with a spoon or the end of a mallet to release the juices from the body cavity. Add the tomato paste and stir to coat the shells. Continue to cook until liquid has been reduced by half and the mixture is pasty.

Add the water and liquid from cooking the lobsters and bring slowly to a simmer. Remove any foam that may rise to the top and discard. Simmer for 35 minutes.

When cool enough to handle, strain the stock through a fine sieve, pressing the solids to remove the maximum amount of stock. Place the stock in a saucepan, bring to a boil, and reduce it to 2 cups to concentrate the flavor. Cool to room temperature.

Lobster Sauce

Makes 2 1/2 cups

3 tablespoons	unsalted butter
1/4 cup	all-purpose flour
2 cups	Lobster Stock
1/2 cup	heavy cream
1 tablespoon	brandy
	Fine sea salt
	White pepper
Pinch	cayenne pepper

Heat 2 tablespoons butter in a saucepan without browning it. Stir in the flour and cook over low heat for 2 minutes, stirring. Add half the lobster stock and whisk vigorously to make a smooth paste. Add the other half of the stock and whisk until smooth. Add the cream and brandy and simmer slowly over low heat for 10 to 15 minutes, whisking occasionally. Stir in the remaining butter. Season to taste with salt, white pepper and cayenne pepper. Remove from heat, allow to cool slightly, and cover with plastic wrap to prevent a skin from forming over the sauce. Reserve until ready to complete the dish.

Creamy White Grits

Makes 12 cups

12 cups	water
3 1/4 cups	coarse stone-ground white grits
1 cup	heavy cream
2 tablespoons	butter
1 tablespoon	salt
1/4 teaspoon	white pepper

Bring the water to a boil in a heavy-bottomed stockpot or large saucepan. Slowly pour in the grits, stirring constantly. Reduce the heat to low and continue to stir so that the grits do not settle to the bottom and scorch. After 8 to 10 minutes, the grits will plump up. Cook the grits very slowly, stirring frequently. Continue to cook the grits over low heat for 30 to 35 minutes, stirring frequently. Add the cream, butter, salt, and white pepper within the last 15 minutes. The grits will have a thick natural creamy consistency and become soft and silky. Keep covered and warm until ready to serve. If the grits become too thick, add warm water to adjust the consistency.

To finish the dish:

3 tablespoons	butter
3 tablespoons	minced shallots
1 1/2 pounds	large sea scallops
1 1/2 pounds	large shrimp, peeled and deveined
	Reserved lobster claw and tail meat cut into bite-size pieces
3 tablespoons	thinly sliced fresh basil

Melt the butter in a large pot without browning it. Add the shallots and cook until translucent. Add the sea scallops and the shrimp. Cook over low heat for 2 to 3 minutes until the scallops are firm but a little translucent in the center and the shrimp are pink. Do not overcook. Add the lobster meat and 2 tablespoons basil and sauté until warm. Add the lobster sauce and heat until warmed throughout. Check seasoning and remove from the heat. Divide the grits between 8 warm bowls and spoon the shellfish in equal amounts over them. Spoon the lobster sauce over the shellfish and garnish with the remaining basil. Serve immediately.

Pan-Fried Grits Cakes

with Sautéed Shrimp, Leeks, and Tomato Gravy

Serves 6 to 8

Grits Cakes

Makes 6 to 8 (2-inch) individual round cakes, 1 1/4 inches thick

6 cups	water
2 1/2 cups	stone-ground grits
1 cup	heavy cream
4 tablespoons	butter
2 teaspoons	salt
Pinch	white pepper

Bring the water to a boil in a heavy-bottomed stockpot or large saucepan. Slowly pour in the grits, stirring constantly. Reduce the heat to low and continue to stir so that the grits do not settle to the bottom and scorch. After 8 to 10 minutes, the grits will plump up. Cook the grits over low heat for 30 to 35 minutes, stirring frequently. Add the cream, butter, salt, and white pepper within the last 15 minutes. The grits will have a thick natural creamy consistency and become soft and silky.

Pour the grits into a 9 x 13-inch pan. If you have to use a different pan, remember that the grits have to be at least 1 1/4 inch thick. Cool to room temperature, cover, and refrigerate. When the grits mixture is set, cut it into the desired shapes, and reserve.

Tomato Gravy

Makes 3 cups

You can finely chop the tomato by hand, blend it with a blender, or use a hand blender.

5 tablespoons	butter
3 tablespoons	all-purpose flour
2 cups	milk
1/4 cup	tomato juice
1 cup	peeled, seeded, and diced fresh tomato
1	bay leaf
2 teaspoons	salt
	White pepper

Heat 2 tablespoons of the butter without browning it. Stir in the flour and cook over very low heat for 3 minutes, stirring. Add half the milk and stir vigorously until the mixture becomes thick and is smooth. Add the rest of the milk and the tomato juice; stir until the mixture thickens again. Add the tomato and the bay leaf and cook over low to medium heat for 15 to 20 minutes, stirring frequently. Skim off any foam that may come to the surface and discard.

Allow the gravy to cook over very low heat for another 10 to 15 minutes, stirring frequently. Season with salt and white pepper. Discard the bay leaf. Whisk in the remaining butter. Adjust the consistency of the gravy with water if it becomes too thick.

Sautéed Shrimp and Leeks

1 cup	cornmeal
1/4 cup	light olive oil
2 tablespoons	butter
1 1/2 cups	sliced and washed leeks
1 pound	medium shrimp, peeled and deveined
	Salt
	Freshly ground black pepper
1/2 cup	chopped fresh parsley

To assemble: Dust the grits cakes with the cornmeal. Heat the olive oil over medium-high heat and pan-fry the grits cakes until they are golden brown on both sides and heated through. Only cook a few at the time so that the oil will stay hot and they won't stick. A Teflon skillet works well. Place onto paper towels and keep warm.

Heat the butter over medium heat, add the leeks, and then cook slowly, without browning, until tender. Add the shrimp and cook until they turn pink, 1 to 2 minutes. Season with salt and pepper to taste.

Place a grits cake on a plate and stack the leeks and shrimp on the cake. Drizzle 3 tablespoons tomato gravy over and around them. Garnish with parsley and serve immediately.

Pimiento Cheese Grits

with Pepper-Seared Sea Scallops and Red Pepper Sauce

This dish brings together five of my favorite ingredients: pimientos, grits, sharp cheddar cheese, sea scallops, and black pepper. The creamy grits take on the flavors of the pimientos and cheddar cheese and make a great accompaniment for the pepper-seared sea scallops.

Serves 6

Pimiento Cheese Grits

Makes 6 cups

6 cups	water
1 2/3 cups	coarse stone-ground white grits
1/2 cup	heavy cream
1 tablespoon	butter
8 ounces	sharp white cheddar cheese
1 cup	roasted, peeled, seeded, and chopped red bell pepper (see p. 36)
1/2 tablespoon	salt
Dash	white pepper

Bring the water to a boil in a heavy-bottomed stockpot or large saucepan. Slowly pour in the grits, stirring constantly. Reduce the heat to low and continue to stir so that the grits do not settle to the bottom and scorch. After 8 to 10 minutes, the grits will plump up. Cook the grits over low heat for another 25 to 30 minutes, stirring frequently. Add the cream, butter, cheese, and the roasted peppers. Cook an additional 10 minutes to melt the cheese and allow peppers to flavor the grits. Season to taste with salt and white pepper. The grits will have a thick natural creamy consistency, and will have become soft and silky. Keep covered and warm until ready to serve. If the grits become too thick, add warm water to adjust the consistency.

Pepper-Seared Sea Scallops

12	large sea scallops
1 tablespoon	freshly ground black pepper
2 teaspoons	fine sea salt
4 tablespoons	light olive oil
2 ounces	white cheddar cheese, cut in small dice for garnish
1/2	recipe Red Pepper Sauce (see p. 53)

Season the sea scallops with the black pepper and salt on the flattest surface of each scallop. Heat the olive oil in a heavy-bottomed frying pan to the smoking point. Gently place the scallops seasoned-side down in the hot oil. Allow them to sear for 1 minute. Carefully lift the scallops so that the oil can get under each one. Continue to sear, adjusting the heat if necessary, until a golden crust or sear is obtained. Gently turn the scallops over and cook them on the other side for 4 to 5 minutes. They should still be a little translucent in the center. Remove from the heat and allow to rest for a moment.

Divide the grits between 6 warm serving plates. Arrange 2 scallops beside the grits and sprinkle with the cheddar cheese and a drizzle of Red Pepper Sauce.

Grilled Salmon Fillet with Dill Butter over Creamy White Grits

I prefer to use fresh dill in this recipe. Dried dill weed can't really provide the same unique fresh taste.

Serves 8

Creamy White Grits

12 cups	water
3 1/4 cups	coarse stone-ground white grits
1 cup	heavy cream
2 tablespoons	butter
1 tablespoon	salt
1/4 teaspoon	white pepper

Bring the water to a boil in a heavy-bottomed stockpot or large saucepan. Slowly pour in the grits, stirring constantly. Reduce the heat to low and continue to stir so that the grits do not settle to the bottom and scorch. After 8 to 10 minutes, the grits will plump up. Cook the grits over low heat for another 30 to 35 minutes, stirring frequently. Add the cream, butter, salt, and white pepper within the last 15 minutes. The grits will have a thick natural creamy consistency and become soft and silky. Keep covered and warm until ready to serve.

If the grits become too thick, add warm water to adjust the consistency. They should be cooked within hours of serving, as they are not the same if reheated after they are refrigerated.

Grilled Salmon with Dill Butter

Fire the grill.

8 (4-ounce)	salmon fillets, skin removed
	Salt
	Freshly ground black pepper
2 tablespoons	light olive oil
1 recipe	Dill Butter (see p. 30)

Season the salmon fillets with salt and pepper and brush them with olive oil. Place them on the grill skin-side up, which is the darker side. Grill the fillets for 3 to 4 minutes per side until they are firm and flake easily when pierced with a fork.

Fill 4 warm bowls with the grits. Place the salmon fillets on top. Place a spoonful of dill butter on top of each fillet and let it melt slightly. Serve immediately.

Chicken Gravy

This very basic velouté sauce makes a great accompaniment to many roasted chicken dishes. If you have pan drippings, adding them will spark the flavor and deepen the color of the gravy. In the Southern kitchen, chicken gravy is served with fried chicken, veal meat loaf and mashed potatoes, or over hot biscuits.

Makes 3¹/₂ cups

4 tablespoons	butter
¹/₂ cup	all-purpose flour
4 cups	Chicken Broth (see p. 17)
2 tablespoons	finely chopped parsley
	Salt
	White pepper

Melt the butter in a heavy-bottomed saucepan over low heat. Make a roux by adding the flour and stirring until well combined. Continue to cook over low heat for 5 minutes, stirring very frequently, until the roux develops a light golden color and has a nutty aroma.

Turn the heat up to medium and gradually add 2 cups of the chicken broth, whisking vigorously. Keep whisking constantly until the broth begins to thicken and is smooth. Gradually add the remaining chicken broth, whisking constantly until the broth thickens into a gravy. Continue to simmer over low heat for 15 minutes to cook out the starchy flavor of the flour. Add the chopped parsley and any pan drippings. Season to taste with salt and white pepper. Serve immediately.

Fish
and
Shellfish

Iron-Skillet Crispy Flounder

with Lemon Caper Aïoli

When my sons and I go fishing and are lucky enough to bring home a flounder or two, this is their favorite way to have it prepared. The little diamonds of fried fish are easily removed with a fork in individual bites with skin that is crispy and flavorful.

I recommend a 15-inch cast iron skillet with about an inch of 340-degree oil. If you have a large fryer with a propane burner and heat the oil to 340 degrees, the entire flounder can be cooked in 7 to 8 minutes.

Serves 2

8 cups	peanut or canola oil
2 cups	all-purpose flour
2 tablespoons	fine sea salt plus some for seasoning
1 tablespoon	white pepper plus some for seasoning
1 (2-pound)	whole flounder, head off, cleaned, and scaled

Use a large enough heavy-bottomed pan that the oil will be only 1 inch deep. Preheat the oil to 340 degrees.

Mix the flour, salt, and white pepper together on a baking sheet with raised edges that is a little bigger than the flounder. Set aside.

With the dark side of the flounder up, use a sharp knife to score the flesh just to the bone with 1-inch parallel cuts at an angle. Be careful not to cut through the bone. Continue to the tail end. Rotate the flounder 90 degrees and score again on an angle to make diamonds. Flip the flounder over and repeat this process on the lighter side.

Season the fish with salt and pepper before dredging it in the seasoned flour. Bend the flounder gently to get some of the seasoning in the areas where it was scored. Dredge it in the seasoned flour, and be sure again that the exposed flesh of the flounder is coated in the flour.

Gently place the floured flounder in the heated oil, dark side down first. Watch over it constantly to control your heat. To prevent burning and allow the fish to cook evenly, give it an occasional lift with a pair of tongs to make sure that there is oil in between the flounder and the skillet. Fry it for 5 to 6 minutes per side, or until it is golden brown and no translucent flesh is apparent in the cuts. Gently turn the flounder over and cook for an additional 3 to 4 minutes. Remove the fish from the skillet, place it on paper towels, and allow it to cool for a few minutes. Serve the fish on a platter, accompanied by the lemon caper aïoli.

Lemon Caper Aïoli

Makes ½ cup

½ cup	mayonnaise
2 tablespoons	minced capers
1 tablespoon	fresh lemon juice
1 teaspoon	chopped fresh parsley
	Salt
Dash	white pepper

Place the mayonnaise in a small mixing bowl, add the capers, lemon juice, and parsley, and incorporate well. Season to taste with salt and white pepper.

Blue Crabs

Just a few quick tips to cooking these local gems: I prefer the Jimmies, which are the large male crabs. A batch of these makes for a great evening of crab picking and conversation amongst friends and family. They taste even better if you've spent the day catching them, not to mention that it keeps the children entertained.

Local spice blends can usually be found where you buy the crabs. Some like to have the spice blend on hand along with melted butter to dip the picked crab in just before eating. Near the Chesapeake Bay area, they add a small dish of distilled white vinegar to their condiment list.

Servers 3 to 4

1/3 bushel	large blue crabs
	Steaming liquid (water, beer, or white vinegar, or a mixture of all three)
2 cups	white vinegar
1 cup	local spice blend or Old Bay seasoning
1/2 pound	butter, melted
	Heavy rubber gloves
	Long tongs
	Steam pot with lid and strainer

Place enough liquid in a steamer to be 1-inch deep. Place over high heat and bring to a boil. Always try to keep the crabs above the liquid level so that they will steam and not boil. Place the live crabs in the steamer basket a few at a time and sprinkle the spice liberally over them. Place a few more crabs, then spice, repeating until the streamer basket is full. Place the basket in the pot and attach the lid firmly. Steam for 18 to 20 minutes for large crabs and 16 to 18 minutes for smaller ones. Turn off heat and carefully remove the lid. Allow for some of the steam to escape before you pull out the steamer basket. Pour onto a table or platter. When cool enough to handle, pick away.

Sautéed Grouper

with Artichoke and Creamy Crabmeat over Sautéed Spinach with Lemon and Leek Butter

Black grouper and many other fish are now being protected in many ways through the efforts of the Sustainable Seafood initiative. It is one of the best quality bottom fish in our local waters, and my preference, but it has become scarce lately. Hopefully, through these conservation efforts, it and all of our local fish will always be available to us.

Serves 4

Artichokes

2 quarts	water
2 tablespoons	light olive oil
1 tablespoon	salt
1	lemon
2	fresh artichokes

Put the water, olive oil, and salt in a non-reactive pot (stainless or porcelain coated). Zest the lemon and reserve both the lemon and the zest. Cut the lemon in half, squeeze the juice into the water, and put the lemon halves into the water also. Pare the artichokes down to the heart, just removing the leaves and keeping the choke intact with the artichoke bottom. Immediately put the artichokes in the water. Place the pot over medium high heat and bring to a simmer. Let the artichokes simmer for 20 to 25 minutes. Remove the pot from the heat and let the artichokes cool in the cooking liquid about 20 minutes, which will allow them to finish cooking.

Remove the artichokes from the water and ease the choke out with your thumb and discard. Return the artichokes to the cooking liquid to hold until ready to use.

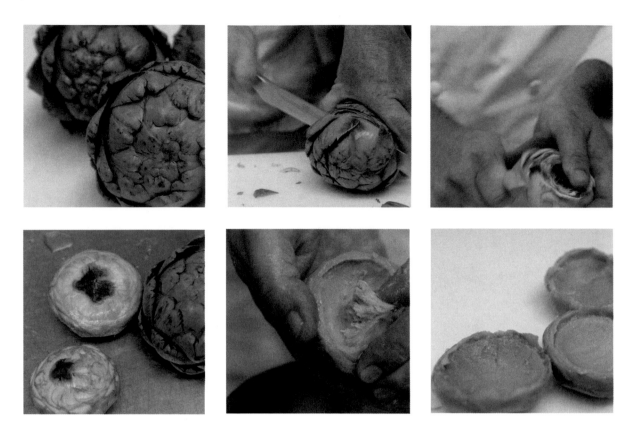

Creamy Crabmeat

½ cup	heavy cream
½ pound	lump crabmeat, gently picked over for shell and drained of any liquid
1 tablespoon	minced chives
	Fine sea salt
	White pepper

Heat the cream in a small saucepan over medium-high heat and reduce it by half. Add the crabmeat and chives. Gently fold them together to warm the crabmeat. Season to taste with salt and white pepper. Keep warm.

Sautéed Spinach

2 tablespoons	butter
12 ounces	baby spinach leaves
	Fine sea salt
	White pepper

Melt the butter in a large frying pan. Add the spinach and cook over medium-low heat until just wilted. Season to taste with salt and white pepper. Drain. Keep warm.

Lemon and Leek Butter

Makes 1 cup

12 tablespoons	unsalted butter	1 teaspoon	lemon zest
1½ cups	leeks, washed and drained very well, ¼-inch dice	Pinch	white pepper
			Fine sea salt
1 tablespoon	white wine	¼ cup	warm water
¼ cup	heavy cream		

Heat 4 tablespoons butter, add the leeks, and cook them for 2 to 3 minutes, or until they have softened. Add the white wine, cook for a moment, then add the cream and reduce by one-third. Add the lemon zest. Gradually whisk in the remaining butter in small amounts over low heat. If the sauce gets too hot, it may separate. The sauce is also at risk if it gets too cold. It should be kept at approximately 120 degrees at all times. When all of the butter is incorporated and melted, the sauce will be thick and creamy. If too thick, adjust the consistency with up to ¼ cup warm water and season with the salt and white pepper to taste. Keep warm.

Sautéed Grouper

4 tablespoons	light olive oil
4 (4- to 5-ounce)	grouper fillets
1 teaspoon	coarse sea salt
½ teaspoon	white pepper
½ cup	all-purpose flour

Preheat an oven to 300 degrees.

Drain the artichoke hearts. Slice each heart vertically into ¼-inch-thick slices.

Heat the olive oil in a heavy ovenproof frying pan until almost smoking. Season the fillets with the salt and white pepper. Lightly dust them in the flour and pat off the excess. Gently place the fillets in the heated oil with the skin-side up. Sauté them for 2 to 3 minutes, lifting the fillets occasionally to let the oil help to cook the fish evenly. Gently turn and sauté the opposite side for an additional 2 to 3 minutes, or until cooked through and the inner flesh of the fillet is white in color with no translucency.

Cover each fillet with a few slices of the artichoke hearts and place in the oven to warm the artichokes for 3 to 4 minutes.

Divide the spinach between 4 warmed plates. Place a fillet of grouper on top of the spinach. Top with the creamy crabmeat. Spoon a few tablespoons of the Lemon and Leek Butter around the spinach and a little over the crabmeat. Serve immediately.

Coriander-Seared Tuna Fillet

with Jalapeño and Mango Vinaigrette, Pan-Fried Potato Cakes, and Sautéed Escarole

The coriander rub adds a pleasing flavor to the tuna and also gives it some texture when it is seared to a golden brown, crusty outer layer. I love the way tuna is complemented by a vinaigrette. This jalapeño and mango vinaigrette is both sweet and a little spicy and has been a favorite on the menu for many years.

Serves 4

Coriander Rub

5 tablespoons	coriander seeds
1 tablespoon	ground ginger
2 tablespoons	freshly ground black pepper
1/4 teaspoon	cayenne pepper
2 tablespoons	coarse sea salt
1/2 cup	light olive oil

Preheat an oven to 350 degrees.

Place the coriander seeds on a baking sheet with raised sides and place in the oven for 5 minutes to toast the seeds and intensify the coriander flavor. Remove and allow the coriander to cool completely. Place the seeds in a spice grinder and pulse until the seeds are pulverized, but not quite a powder. Put the coriander, ginger, black pepper, cayenne pepper, sea salt, and olive oil in a small bowl and mix well to combine. Reserve.

Tuna

4 (5- to 6-ounce)	tuna fillets
4 tablespoons	coriander rub

Rub the tuna fillets with the coriander rub on all sides. Cover and refrigerate for at least 3 hours, or overnight.

Jalapeño and Mango Vinaigrette

Makes 1 1/2 cups

2 tablespoons	Dijon mustard
2 tablespoons	cider vinegar
1/4 cup	fresh lemon juice
1 cup	light olive oil
2 tablespoons	chopped chives
1 teaspoon	minced garlic
1 tablespoon	minced jalapeño pepper
3/4 cup	diced mango
1/4 teaspoon	freshly ground black pepper

Place the mustard, vinegar, and lemon juice in a bowl and whisk them together. Add the olive oil very slowly in a steady stream, whisking vigorously until the oil is incorporated. Add the chives, garlic, jalapeño, mango, and pepper and stir to combine. Reserve at room temperature.

Pan-Fried Potato Cakes

2 cups	peeled russet potatoes, cut in equal-size pieces
3 cups	water
1 1/2 teaspoons	salt
2 tablespoons	butter
1/4 cup	finely diced onion
1 teaspoon	minced garlic
2 tablespoons	heavy cream
1/8 teaspoon	white pepper
1 tablespoon	minced fresh parsley
1/2 cup	panko, (see p. 154) plus additional for dusting cakes
1/4 cup	light olive oil

Place the potatoes, water, and 1 teaspoon salt in a saucepan over medium heat. Bring to a boil and cook for 18 to 20 minutes, or until the potatoes are tender. Drain off the water and place the pan back over the heat for 1 minute, stirring constantly to steam-dry the potatoes. This helps to get a little of the excessive moisture out.

Heat the butter in a small saucepan. Add the onion and garlic and cook for
1 minute without browning. Add the cream, remaining salt, and the white
pepper and warm. Pour into the cooked potato mixture and mix gently to
combine. Add the parsley and the panko, mix into the potato mixture, and
allow for it to absorb. Shape into 1/2-cup size cakes that are at least 11/4 inches
thick. Dust with the additional panko.

Preheat an oven to 200 degrees.

Heat the olive oil in a heavy-bottomed frying pan over medium-high heat and
sauté the potato cakes until they are golden on both sides and heated
through. Place in the oven to keep warm.

Sautéed Escarole

2 tablespoons	light olive oil
6 cups	roughly chopped escarole, washed and dried
1 teaspoon	minced garlic
	Salt
	Freshly ground black pepper

Heat the oil in a large heavy-bottomed frying pan over medium heat. Add the
escarole and toss gently until it begins to wilt. Add the garlic and continue to
cook for 2 minutes. Season with salt and pepper to taste. Keep warm.

To finish the dish, heat 2 tablespoons light olive oil in a heavy-bottomed sauté
pan over medium-high heat. Carefully place the tuna fillets in the heated oil and
sear until they get a crusty appearance. Gently turn them over and sauté for 2 1/2
to 3 minutes for medium rare.

Place the warm potato cakes into the center of 4 warmed plates and place
some of the cooked escarole around them. Place the seared tuna on the
potato cakes and spoon some of the vinaigrette over and around the tuna.
Serve immediately.

Fire-Roasted Cedar-Planked Salmon

This is a great dish that takes a little preparation. I like to serve the salmon right on the plank that it is cooked on. When you are ready to serve it, simply invert the plank and snip off the wire at each revolution. Discard the wire. Using a fork, flake the salmon into large pieces and serve immediately. Any selection of the compound butters recommended for fish in this book will work well with this fire-roasted salmon.

Serves 10 to 12

1 (2 1/2- to 3-pound)	salmon fillet with the skin attached
1/3 cup	coarse sea salt
1 bunch	fresh rosemary
1 bunch	fresh thyme
2 tablespoons	freshly ground black pepper
1	cedar plank, 8 inches wide and at least 5 feet long
2	small nails or screws
15 feet	metal wire
1 pair	wire cutters
	Seasoned oak, hickory, or your choice of hardwood for the fire
	Fire resistant supports to hold the plank over the coals

Start your fire a couple of hours ahead of time so that you have a bed of coals as wide as the fillet is long. Prepare the plank by toasting it over the hot coals until it begins to blacken slightly. Allow the cedar to cool. Place the plank so that it rests with a support on either end and the toasted side up. Sprinkle it with a little coarse sea salt. Place the salmon fillet on the plank skin-side down. Tap one of the nails into one of the narrow sides of the plank about 3 inches from the front of the fillet. Repeat with the other nail a few inches past the tail. Season the top side of the salmon with the remaining salt and pepper. Lay the rosemary and thyme sprigs lengthwise on the fillet. Starting at the large end of the fillet, twist the wire around the nail a time or two until you are sure that it will hold. Wrap the wire entirely around the salmon, herb sprigs and the plank repeatedly, keeping the wraps no more than 2 inches apart. The wraps should be fairly tight, but not so tight that they slice through the tender flesh of the salmon. Continue until the length of the salmon is secure and then twist the wire around the second nail on the tail side. Trim off excess wire.

Arrange your plank supports near the fire. Place the plank, salmon-side down approximately 15 to 20 inches above the hot coals. It is best that the salmon roasts slowly at first. Try not to scorch the herbs before the salmon cooks. The longer the salmon cooks, the better the roasted flavor. The oils of the salmon will be released and the flesh of the salmon should caramelize slightly. This imparts a great flavor and texture to the salmon. The cooking time will vary due to the heat of the fire and the distance the salmon is kept from the fire. Roast the salmon for 25 to 35 minutes, or until the thicker section of the fillet feels firm to the touch.

Squash Blossoms with Scallop and Lobster Mousse and Lobster Sauce

We always look forward to the early summer months when the local farmers come around with these beautiful, delicate blossoms, some of which are still attached to their fruit.

If you don't have a pastry bag, it is just as easy to use a one-gallon zipper-lock bag. Put the mousse into the bag, gently move it into one corner, snip off the corner tip of the bag, and pipe into the blossoms.

Serves 6

Lobsters

1 (2-pound)   live Maine lobster

Lobsters will yield approximately 28 percent of their overall weight when they are cooked and the meat is removed. This 2-pound lobster should yield at least $1/2$ pound of succulent meat. By making the stock from the shells, then the sauce from the stock, the wonderful result is this buttery lobster sauce, which is actually the same as a classic lobster bisque.

Bring 3 cups water to a boil in a large pot with a tight-fitting lid. Place the lobster on its back and pierce through the head between its legs with a sturdy knife tip. Place the lobster in the pot, cover and steam for 6 to 7 minutes. Meanwhile, prepare an ice bath. Remove the lobster and immerse it totally in the ice bath to cool. Reserve the pot and the steaming liquid. When the lobster is cool enough to handle, remove the claws and the tail over the pot in order to catch all of the juices. Reserve the meat, the shells, and the liquid in the pot.

Lightly tap the claws to just crack the shells. Remove the claw meat as much intact as possible. Lay the tail on its sides and tap lightly to crack the shell. Remove the tail meat as much intact as possible. Remove the intestinal tract along the back of the tail meat and discard. Reserve all of the shells. Place the lobster meat in a bowl and refrigerate.

Lobster Stock

Makes 4 cups

2 tablespoons	light olive oil		1	bay leaf
1/3 cup	chopped onion		2	black peppercorns, crushed
1/3 cup	chopped celery		1/2 teaspoon	fine sea salt
1/4 cup	chopped carrot			Reserved lobster shells
1	garlic clove, smashed		3 ounces	tomato paste
2	sprigs fresh tarragon		4 cups	water
3	leaves fresh basil			Reserved steaming liquid

Heat the oil in a heavy-bottomed pot. Add the onion, celery, and carrot and cook over low heat until the vegetables are soft, but not caramelized. Add the garlic, tarragon, basil, bay leaf, peppercorns and salt. Cook for 1 minute. Add the shells and crush them with a spoon or the end of a mallet to release the juices from the body cavity. Add the tomato paste and stir to coat the shells. Continue to cook until the liquid has been reduced by half and the mixture is pasty.

Add the water and liquid from cooking the lobster and bring slowly to a simmer. Remove any foam that may rise to the top and discard. Simmer for 35 minutes.

When cool enough to handle, strain the stock through a fine sieve, pressing the solids to extract the maximum amount of stock. Place the stock in a saucepan, bring to a boil, and reduce it to 1 1/2 cups to concentrate the flavor. Cool to room temperature.

Lobster Sauce

Makes 1 1/2 cups

2 tablespoons	unsalted butter
2 tablespoons	all-purpose flour
1 1/2 cups	lobster stock
1/4 cup	heavy cream
2 teaspoons	brandy
1/2 teaspoon	fine sea salt
	White pepper
Pinch	cayenne pepper

Heat 1 tablespoon butter in a saucepan without browning it. Stir in the flour and cook over low heat for 2 minutes, stirring. Add half the lobster stock and whisk vigorously to make a smooth paste. Add the remaining stock and whisk until smooth. Add the cream and brandy and simmer slowly over low heat for 8 to 10 minutes, whisking occasionally. Stir in the remaining butter and the salt. Season to taste with white pepper and cayenne pepper. Remove from heat, allow to cool slightly, and cover with plastic wrap to prevent a skin from forming over the sauce. Reserve until ready to finish the dish.

Mousse and Squash Blossoms

1/2 pound	sea scallops, very cold
3/4 cup	heavy cream, very cold
1/4 teaspoon	salt
Pinch	cayenne pepper
Pinch	white pepper
1/2 pound	lobster meat, cut into 1/2 inch pieces
2 tablespoons	sliced chives
12	yellow squash or zucchini blossoms
	butter

Place the bowl and the steel blade of a food processor in the freezer until very cold. Remove it from the freezer and place the scallops in it. Pulse until the scallops are roughly chopped. Scrape down the bowl with a rubber spatula. With the motor running, stream in half the cream. Scrape down the bowl. Repeat the process with the remaining cream. Scrape down the bowl again and process to make smooth. The total preparation time should only take 1 to 1 1/2 minutes. The mixture should be smooth, shiny and cold. The processor should only run long enough to incorporate the cream. Otherwise, the heat produced by the friction of the high-speed processor will break down the mousse and a grainy, undesirable texture will result.

Transfer the mousse into a chilled bowl and, using a rubber spatula, fold in the salt, cayenne pepper, white pepper, lobster meat, and 1 tablespoon chives. Put the mousse into a pastry bag or zipper-lock bag and refrigerate.

A quick dip in room temperature water and a gentle shake should clean the blossoms of any possible sand or dirt that may be present. Gently stick your finger into the blossoms and break off the center of the flower (stigma) and discard. Place the tip of the piping bag into the blossom and pipe in the mousse until the blossom fills out, slowly pulling the bag out of the blossom as it fills. Allow the tips of the petals to conceal the mousse in a natural way.

Lightly butter a steamer. Steam the blossoms for 5 to 6 minutes. The mousse within the blossom should be firm. Spoon the Lobster Sauce onto the plates, place the blossoms on top of the sauce, and garnish with the remaining chives. Serve immediately.

Seared Tuna Fillets

with Carolina Aromatic Rice and Warm Salad of Artichoke, Lemon, Leek, and Capers

This tuna dish is Mediterranean style and heart-healthy, with no butter used. It all comes together nicely with the aromatic rice, artichoke salad, olive oil, balsamic vinegar, and a little sprinkle of coarse sea salt. Even though artichokes are not indigenous to the South, I love to cook with this versatile vegetable.

Serves 4

Artichokes (see p. 136)

Warm Salad of Artichoke, Lemon, Leek, and Capers

This recipe works best with leeks that are 3/4 to 1-inch in diameter.

1 cup	circular leek slices, cut 3/8 inch thick
4 tablespoons	highest quality extra-virgin olive oil
1 tablespoon	garlic cloves, sliced into very thin slices
1 teaspoon	reserved lemon zest
	Artichoke bottoms, sliced 1/4 inch thick
1/2 cup	lightly packed Italian parsley leaves
2 tablespoons	capers
	Coarse sea salt
	Freshly ground black pepper

Wash the leeks well, but try to keep the slices intact. Heat 2 tablespoons olive oil in a heavy-bottomed pan over low heat. Add the leeks and cook for 1 minute. Add the garlic and cook until soft. Do not brown. Add 1/2 teaspoon lemon zest, artichokes, parsley, and capers. Season to taste with the salt and pepper. Remove the pan from the heat, drizzle with the remaining olive oil, and toss gently. Loosely cover and keep warm.

Tuna

4 (4- to 5-ounce)	tuna fillets about 1¼ inches thick
1 tablespoon	coarse sea salt
1 tablespoon	freshly ground black pepper
⅓ cup	light olive oil

Season the tuna with the sea salt and pepper on both sides of the fillet. Heat the olive oil in a heavy-bottomed sauté pan over medium-high heat. Carefully sear the fillets until they are golden brown. Gently turn them over and cook for 2½ to 3 minutes for medium rare.

To finish:

1 recipe	Carolina Aromatic Rice (see p. 95)
½ cup	highest quality extra-virgin olive oil
½ cup	aged balsamic vinegar, reduced to ¼ cup over medium heat and cooled
	Coarse sea salt

Place about ¼ cup cooked rice on the plate, place the warm salad around the rice, and place the tuna on top of the rice. Drizzle the olive oil and balsamic vinegar around the outer edges of the warm salad. Sprinkle with a little coarse sea salt and the reserved lemon zest. Serve immediately.

Broiled Rock Shrimp

with Garlic Butter and Parmesan

These shrimp are like tiny little lobster tails. I always have to buy them when I see them available in the market. Simply split them open from the underside, drizzle with the garlic butter, sprinkle with Parmigiano-Reggiano, and broil.

Serves 4

2 pounds	rock shrimp, shells on, heads off

Garlic Butter

8 tablespoons	butter, room temperature
2 tablespoons	minced garlic
1 tablespoon	minced fresh parsley
1 cup	freshly grated Parmigiano-Reggiano
1	lemon, cut into wedges
	Parsley sprigs for garnish

Place the butter, garlic, and minced parsley in a small saucepan over low heat and melt the butter.

Holding the rock shrimp with the back of the shell on the cutting board, place a knife tip between the legs near the tail. Cut between the legs towards the head end of the shrimp to butterfly it open. It is important not to completely slice through the shell. Spread the shell open so that it will remain that way. Place the shrimp on a baking sheet with raised sides, "head to tail," until all of the shrimp are split. Remove the intestinal tracts of the split shrimp with a pair of tweezers.

Drizzle the shrimp with half of the garlic butter and sprinkle them with the grated cheese. Broil them under a hot broiler for 2 to 3 minutes, rotating the baking sheet halfway through the cooking.

Place 10 of the rock shrimp on each plate with the tails turned to the center of the plate. Drizzle with the remaining half of the garlic butter. Garnish with lemon wedges and parsley sprigs.

Carolina Crab Cakes

with Tomato Gravy, Creamed Corn, and Sautéed Spinach

At Magnolias, we serve the crab cakes with Tomato Gravy (see p. 122), Creamed Corn (see p. 101), and Sautéed Spinach. This makes a colorful and tasty combination.

All crabmeat should be picked over to remove any possible remaining shell, but do it gently because you don't want to break up the lumps. Then place the crabmeat in a strainer and press down lightly to extract any extra liquid.

Panko, frequently referred to as Japanese bread crumbs, is coarser than American bread crumbs. Panko is available in most grocery stores in the Asian section. It creates a very golden and crunchy breading when dipping and frying, and also works well as a binder. You may prefer to lightly dust the crab cakes in panko to give the cakes a crispy golden crust. The crumbs are very neutral in flavor and light in color.

Makes 8 (3-ounce) cakes

½ cup	finely minced red onions
⅓ cup	finely minced red bell pepper
1 tablespoon	minced fresh tarragon
⅓ cup	mayonnaise
1 pound	jumbo lump or lump crabmeat, gently picked over and drained of any liquid
¾ cup	panko
2 teaspoons	salt
¼ teaspoon	white pepper
⅛ teaspoon	cayenne pepper
6 tablespoons	light olive oil

Place onions, bell pepper, tarragon, and mayonnaise in a mixing bowl and combine. Gently fold in the crabmeat. Add the panko and season with salt, white pepper, and cayenne pepper to taste. Let the mixture rest for 5 minutes. The panko will absorb some of the moisture and the mixture will stay together.

Lay out a large piece of plastic wrap on a clean counter surface. Place half of the crab mixture on it and use a spatula or a spoon to form it into a tube about 1 3/4 inches in diameter. Bring the wrap up over the crab and roll the crab mixture up. Twist the ends to close. Pierce any air pockets with a toothpick or skewer. Twist the ends even tighter to compress the crab mixture. Tuck under the ends of the wrap and place the tube on a plate. Repeat with the second half of the crab cake mixture. Place the tubes in the refrigerator for at least 1 hour or overnight.

Note: If you don't want to go through the process of making the tubes, form the mixture into 8 equal size 3-ounce cakes by hand or with a scoop. Refrigerate for 30 minutes before cooking.

Preheat an oven to 350 degrees.

When ready to use, cut the tubes into 1 1/4-inch-thick cakes. Gently remove the plastic wrap, leaving the cakes in nice cylinders. Heat 3 tablespoons oil in a heavy-bottomed frying pan over medium-high heat until very hot, but not smoking. Gently place 4 of the crab cakes in the pan and sear for 3 to 4 minutes or until golden brown. Gently turn the cakes over and sear 3 to 4 minutes, or until golden brown. Place them on a baking sheet. Wipe the pan, add the remaining olive oil, and repeat this process for the other 4 crab cakes.

Sautéed Spinach

3 tablespoons	butter
1 pound	baby spinach leaves, washed and dried
Pinch	salt
Dash	white pepper

Heat the butter in a large heavy-bottomed frying pan. Add the spinach and cook over medium-low heat until just wilted. Season to taste with salt and white pepper. Drain. Keep warm.

Serve the crab cakes with Tomato Gravy (see p. 122), Creamed Corn (see p. 101), and a small amount of the Sautéed Spinach.

Buttermilk and Beer Batter–Fried Soft-Shell Crabs

This is nature's way for us to enjoy the whole crab without any fear of handling these little devils or the painstaking process of picking their sweet meat from the ever-present shell. Here are three of the many ways to serve these delicacies. My personal favorite is the batter-dipped legs and claws. They make an excellent finger food or hors d'oeuvres.

The beer batter may also be used for shrimp. It will batter about 3 pounds of medium shrimp that are peeled and deveined but have their tails conveniently left on.

Serves 8

8	soft-shell crabs
1/2 cup	buttermilk
2	eggs
1 1/2 cups	all-purpose flour
1 1/2 teaspoons	aluminum-free baking powder
2 tablespoons	sugar
2 teaspoons	salt
2 teaspoons	freshly ground black pepper
1 teaspoon	dried thyme
1 teaspoon	dried oregano
1 teaspoon	dried basil
10 ounces	beer
1 tablespoon	Worcestershire sauce
12 cups	peanut oil or canola oil
	Salt
	Freshly ground black pepper
1 cup	all-purpose flour for dusting crabs

Remove the gills on the left and right sides of the top of the crab by lifting up each side of the shell. Peel them back and snip off with scissors. These are known as "the dead man's fingers." Remove the skirt located at the bottom of the crab. Trim off the face. Keep cold.

Preheat an oven to 225 degrees.

Beat together the buttermilk and eggs. Combine the flour, baking powder, sugar, salt, black pepper, thyme, oregano, and basil. Slowly sprinkle half the flour and herb mixture into the buttermilk and egg mixture, whisking into a smooth paste. Add the remaining flour and herb mixture and whisk until smooth. Slowly add the beer, whisking until the mixture is smooth. The mixture should be thick and batter-like. Whisk in the Worcestershire sauce. Season with salt and pepper.

Gradually heat the oil over medium-high to 350 degrees. To fry the crabs whole, you do not have to precook the crabs. Dust the crabs with the flour. Shake off any excess. Holding the crabs by their two back fins, immerse in the batter. Then carefully immerse into the hot oil, two whole crabs at a time. They may spit and splatter, so have a splatter guard handy. Keep the oil at 350 degrees. Fry the crabs until they are golden brown, remove the crabs from the oil, and place on paper towels to absorb any excess oil. You may hold the crabs in a 225-degree oven until all are fried. Serve at once with Honey Mustard Dip.

Hors d'oeuvres

Season and flour the crabs. Sauté them in hot olive oil for 1 to 2 minutes on each side. Remove the crabs from the pan and refrigerate to cool quickly. Pull off the claws and the top shell. Cut the body of the crab down the center. Then cut it across between the four legs. You should have six pieces per crab: two claws and four leg pieces.

Heat the peanut or canola oil to 350 degrees, as above. Working with 2 pieces at a time, use the claw and leg ends as handles and dip the meat end into the flour. Shake off any excess flour. Immerse the pieces into the batter. Carefully place them in the hot oil. The pieces may spit and splatter, so have a splatter guard handy. Keep the oil at 350 degrees. Fry the pieces until they are golden brown. Remove the pieces from the oil and place on paper towels to absorb the excess oil. Serve at once with the Honey Mustard Dip.

Spicy Soft-Shell Crabs

Dredge the cleaned crabs in Magnolias' Blackening Spice (see p. 21) and sauté them in olive oil over medium-high heat for about 2 minutes on each side.

Honey Mustard Dip

Makes 1½ cups

1 cup	honey
½ cup	Dijon mustard
1 teaspoon	chopped fresh parsley

Combine the honey, mustard, and parsley and mix well. Use at once or put in a storage container, cover, and refrigerate.

Lowcountry Bouillabaisse

Local fish and shellfish, sweet corn, spicy pot liquor, and tasso give this classic dish Down South connotations.

Serves 6

Pot Liquor

Makes 2 quarts

2 tablespoons	light olive oil
½ cup	yellow corn kernels
2 tablespoons	finely chopped jalapeño pepper
2 tablespoons	roughly chopped garlic
4	thyme sprigs
2	bay leaves
1 teaspoon	red chili flakes
2 cups	white wine
6 cups	clam juice
6 cups	tomato juice
2 cups	water
Pinch	saffron threads
	Fine sea salt
	Freshly ground black pepper

Heat the olive oil over medium heat in a heavy-bottomed soup pot. Add the corn, jalapeños, garlic, thyme sprigs, bay leaves, and chili flakes. Cook for 1 minute without browning. Add the white wine and cook for 3 minutes. Add the clam juice, tomato juice, and water. Increase the heat to medium-high and bring to a boil. Reduce to a simmer, remove any foam that may appear, and discard. Add the saffron. Reduce the pot liquor by one-third to one-half of its volume. Season to taste with salt and pepper. Strain through a sieve. Reserve warm for immediate use or cool to room temperature, place in a storage container, cover, and refrigerate.

Croutons

4	bias-cut French baguette slices, 1/4-inch thick
2 tablespoons	butter

Spread the bread with the butter and toast under a broiler or on a grill until golden and crispy.

Bouillabaisse

3 tablespoons	light olive oil
3/4 cup	cooked corn kernels
1/4 cup	diced red bell peppers, cut in 1/4 inch dice
1/4 cup	diced celery, cut in 1/4 inch dice
1/4 cup	diced red onion, cut in 1/4 inch dice
1/4 cup	diced tasso, cut in 1/4 inch dice
1 dozen	clams, scrubbed and washed well
1 cup	white wine
2 quarts	pot liquor
18	mussels, scrubbed and debearded
18	large shrimp, peeled and deveined
1 pound	white fish, such as grouper or snapper, cut in 1-inch pieces
1 cup	diced cooked new potatoes, skin on
2 tablespoons	minced fresh parsley
1 teaspoon	sea salt
1 teaspoon	black pepper

In a large saucepan with a lid, heat the olive oil over medium-high heat. Add the corn kernels, peppers, celery, red onion, and tasso. Cook for 3 to 4 minutes, stirring frequently, until the vegetables become soft and the tasso spices are released. Add the clams and stir for 2 minutes to start the cooking process. Add the white wine and 1 cup pot liquor. Increase the heat to high and cover. Steam for 6 to 7 minutes. Reduce the heat to medium. Carefully remove the lid and add the mussels, shrimp, fish, and potatoes. Add enough pot liquor to cover the surface of the shellfish. Cover and poach for 6 to 8 minutes, or until the fish and shrimp are cooked through and the mussels are open. An occasional gentle stir may be necessary. Add 1 tablespoon parsley, the salt, and the pepper.

Divide the seafood equally among 6 large serving bowls. Ladle some of the pot liquor with the vegetables and tasso over it. Sprinkle with the remaining parsley, place a crouton on each dish and serve immediately.

Meats and Poultry

Hickory Smoked Pork Shoulder

with Carolina Barbecue Sauce, Crackling Cream Biscuits, and Spicy Yellow Corn

Start your pork shoulder with the rub the day before because you will need to begin cooking it early in the morning.

Serves 6 to 8

1   (6- to 7-pound) pork shoulder

Dry Rub

2 teaspoons	granulated garlic powder
1 teaspoon	cumin
3 teaspoons	freshly ground black pepper
1/2 teaspoon	cayenne pepper
2 teaspoons	granulated onion powder
2 1/2 teaspoons	salt

Mix all of the ingredients together. Rub the entire shoulder with 3/4 of the spice mixture and refrigerate for at least 1 hour, or overnight. Reserve the remaining rub.

Place the shoulder in a grill or smoker with hickory chips or chunks that is preheated to 265 degrees and has smoke present. Place the pork indirectly over the heat source and smoke it for 5 to 7 hours, or until the shoulder reaches an internal temperature of 185 degrees for sliced pork shoulder and 190 degrees for pulled pork shoulder. If you are using wood chips and a grill, the chips should be soaked and applied about every 40 minutes.

When the shoulder has reached the desired temperature, remove the meat, and allow it to rest for 10 to 15 minutes. Use immediately or cool to room temperature, cover, and refrigerate overnight.

Carolina Barbecue Sauce

Makes 3 cups

2 cups	cider vinegar
1½ cups	apple cider
1 cup	dark brown sugar
2 tablespoons	yellow mustard seeds
2 tablespoons	Dijon mustard
½ cup	tomato paste
¼ teaspoon	salt
¼ teaspoon	freshly ground black pepper
2	smoked pork neck bones or ham hocks

Combine all of the ingredients in a heavy-bottomed saucepan. Place over medium heat and allow to cook slowly for 30 to 40 minutes, or until the sauce thickens. Remove any foam that may appear on the surface of the sauce as it cooks and discard it. Check the seasoning. Remove the neck bones or hocks and allow the sauce to cool to room temperature. Check the seasoning and use immediately or put into a storage container, cool to room temperature, cover, and refrigerate.

Crackling Cream Biscuits

Makes 24 (1-inch) biscuits

2½ cups	White Lily self-rising flour
2 cups	heavy cream
4 tablespoons	Carolina Ham Cracklings (see p. 22)
2 tablespoons	coarse sea salt
3 tablespoons	melted butter

Preheat an oven to 400 degrees.

Place the flour in a mixing bowl. Add 1½ cups cream to the flour until it starts to come together and is a wet sticky dough. Add 2 tablespoons cracklings and work together for a minute or so. Place on a lightly floured surface and press or roll the dough out to less than ½ inch thick. Brush the top of the biscuit dough with the remaining cream. This is to assist in holding the cracklings and salt on the biscuit after baking. Sprinkle the remaining cracklings and the sea salt on the top of the dough and gently press down. Cut the biscuits with a 1-inch biscuit cutter. Place on an ungreased baking sheet and bake 8 to 10 minutes, or until golden. Remove from the oven, brush with the melted butter, and serve immediately.

Spicy Yellow Corn

1 tablespoon	light olive oil
2 cups	fresh corn kernels
2 tablespoons	Carolina Ham Cracklings (see p. 22)
	Dry Rub

Heat the oil in a pan and add the corn kernels. Allow the kernels to caramelize over medium heat. Add the cracklings and season to taste with the Dry Rub.

Warm the pork in a small amount of the sauce to moisten and season it. Divide between the plates and place 3 of the biscuits around it. Drizzle with more of the sauce and then sprinkle with the corn. Serve immediately.

Pork Barbecue Sliders

with Classic Potato Fries

There are many different ways to cook this Southern favorite and many different pieces of equipment that could be used. Because the key is to cook slowly over low heat—although not under 200 degrees—with a small amount of smoke, my favorite way is to grill it, but I'm also including an oven method for this mouth-watering treat. We serve the sliders on soft square dinner rolls, which you should be able to purchase at your local bakery or grocery store.

Makes 2 ½ pounds

1	(6- to 7-pound) pork shoulder
3 to 4 tablespoons	Sweet and Hot Pork Shoulder and Rib Rub (see p. 20)
	Classic Potato Fries (see p. 92)

To cook on a grill or smoker, see the instructions for Hickory Smoked Pork Shoulder (see p. 166).

To cook in the oven, preheat an oven to 350 degrees.

Rub the pork with the Rib Rub. Place the pork in the oven and roast for 1 hour. Lower the temperature to 210 degrees and continue to roast for about 10 hours until the internal temperature of 190 degrees is reached, at which point the meat is done and tender enough to pull apart.

Save the juice to put in the Barbecue Sauce, using the following procedure: Remove as much of the grease as you can from the roasting pan. Deglaze the pan with a little water. Pour this into a container and put it into the refrigerator. When the grease comes to the top and solidifies, remove it and use the pure juice to give more depth and flavor to the sauce.

With either method, after the pork is cool enough to handle, pull the meat apart, discarding the shoulder bone, if present, and any pockets of heavy fat. Lightly chop the meat and put it in a skillet over low heat. Moisten the tender meat with some of the Barbecue Sauce and place between soft dinner rolls that have been pulled apart and warmed in the oven to lightly toast the edges. Serve with the Classic Potato Fries.

Barbecue Sauce

This is a cross between a mopping sauce and a more traditional barbecue sauce. It works well with any pork, ribs, or chicken. It can be heated and tossed with freshly pulled pork barbecue or served in a bowl on the side. Add the pan drippings from the roasted pork if you cook it in the oven. If you desire a less tangy sauce, only use 3/4 cup of the cider vinegar and add 3/4 cup Chicken Broth (see p. 17).

1 1/2 cups	cider vinegar
1/4 cup	Dijon mustard
1 cup	ketchup
2 tablespoons	Worcestershire sauce
1 teaspoon	freshly ground black pepper
1 tablespoon	Tabasco sauce
1/4 cup	blackstrap molasses
2 tablespoons	dark brown sugar

Combine all of the ingredients in a heavy-bottomed saucepan over medium heat. Simmer them for 5 minutes to meld the flavors. The sauce should be just thick enough to coat a spoon. Use at once or let cool at room temperature, cover, and refrigerate. The barbecue sauce will keep for about a week in the refrigerator if it has pan drippings in it or for several weeks if it does not.

Herb-Seared Lamb Loin

with Natural Jus, Butter-Whipped Potatoes, and Sautéed Spinach

This recipe for loin of lamb is very easy because everything except cooking the loin can be done ahead of time. I recommend serving this with our Butter-Whipped Potatoes (see p. 93) and Sautéed Spinach (see p. 138).

Serves 2

Lamb

1   (1½-pound) rack of lamb

Trim off the excess fat right down to the membrane covering the loin. With the tip of a knife, remove the loin from the rib bones, reserving the bones and being careful to not cut into the loin. The trimmed, boneless loin should weigh about 12 ounces.

Marinade

1 teaspoon	minced garlic
1 teaspoon	peeled, minced ginger
1 teaspoon	minced fresh rosemary
1 teaspoon	minced fresh sage
1 teaspoon	minced fresh thyme
¼ teaspoon	freshly ground black pepper
½ teaspoon	light olive oil

Mix the ingredients to make a marinade. Rub the boneless loin with the marinade. The loin can be cooked right after it is rubbed or it can be refrigerated for several hours or overnight.

Jus

1 teaspoon	light olive oil
	Lamb ribs reserved from trimming the rack of lamb, cut into individual ribs
½ cup	roughly chopped yellow onion
1 teaspoon	minced garlic
¼ cup	roughly chopped ginger

¼ cup	roughly chopped carrot
¼ cup	roughly chopped celery
1 tablespoon	fresh rosemary
1	bay leaf
4	peppercorns
6	parsley stems
1 tablespoon plus 1 teaspoon	tomato paste
2 cups	Chicken Broth (see p. 17)
	Salt
	Freshly ground black pepper

Heat the olive oil in a heavy-bottomed pan over medium-high heat until the oil is
 smoking. Add the lamb ribs and sear them for 3 to 5 minutes, stirring frequently
 so that they brown evenly. Add the onion, garlic, ginger, carrot, celery, rosemary,
 bay leaf, peppercorns, and parsley stems and continue to brown the mixture for
 another 3 or 5 minutes. Add the tomato paste and cook for 1 minute.

Add the chicken broth and deglaze the pan, scraping up all of the browned bits for
 color and flavor. Gently simmer this mixture for 8 to 10 minutes to reduce the liquid
 volume by half, removing any foam that may appear on top. Strain the mixture
 through a very fine sieve or strainer and season to taste with salt and pepper.
 Discard the ribs and solids. Use immediately or place in a storage container, cool
 to room temperature, cover, and refrigerate.

To cook the lamb:

> ½ teaspoon   light olive oil

Preheat an oven to 350 degrees.

Heat the olive oil in an oven-proof pan over medium-high heat until the oil is smoking. Gently lay the loin in the oil and sear for 4 to 5 minutes, turning so that all
 the sides are browned evenly. You want to achieve a crisp, seared crust. Place the
 pan in the oven for approximately:

> 5 to 6 minutes for medium rare
> 8 to 9 minutes for medium
> 15 minutes for well done

Remove the pan from the oven. Place the loin on a plate and allow it to rest for
 5 minutes. Place on a cutting board, slice the loin into thin slices, and divide them
 between 2 warmed plates. Drizzle with some of the lamb jus. Serve immediately.

Grilled Filet of Beef Topped with Pimiento Cheese

and Served with Grilled Tomatoes, Green Onions, Parsley Potatoes, and Madeira Sauce

At Magnolias, we spoon some of the Madeira Sauce on each warm plate, then add the filets, potatoes, tomatoes, and onions. The pimiento cheese warms and makes a colorful topping. The combination of flavors, textures, and colors makes this an outstanding dish.

Serves 4

4	(6- to 8-ounce) filets of beef
2 tablespoons	light olive oil
	Salt
	Freshly ground black pepper
	Pimiento Cheese (see p. 35)
	Grilled tomatoes
	Grilled green onions
	Parsley Potatoes (see p. 94)
	Madeira Sauce

Fire the grill.

Brush the filets with olive oil and sprinkle with salt and pepper. Place the filets on the hot grill, close the lid, and cook to just below the desired temperature. Depending on the intensity of your grill, a filet should cook about 8 to 10 minutes per side to reach medium rare, which registers at 120 to 125 degrees on a meat thermometer. There are, however, a number of varying factors in how long to cook the filet: the thickness of the meat, the exact weight of the meat, and the heat of the grill. This is why a meat thermometer is helpful.

When you get close to your desired temperature, take the filets off the grill. Spread the top of each filet with 2 or 3 tablespoons of pimiento cheese. Place the filets back on the grill, close the lid, and cook for another 2 to 3 minutes. Serve immediately.

Grilled Tomatoes and Green Onions

1 teaspoon	olive oil
1 teaspoon	minced garlic
1/8 teaspoon	freshly ground black pepper
Dash	salt

Whisk together, making a marinade.

Grilled tomatoes: Cut 2 Roma tomatoes in half. Rub with the marinade. Grill 3 to 4 minutes, gently turning once.

Green onions: Toss 1 bunch of 6 to 8 onions, roots and tips of green ends removed, with the marinade. Grill for about 2 minutes, turning so that all sides are grilled and they become limp.

Veal Stock

5 pounds	veal bones, cut into small pieces
	Light olive oil
6 ounces	tomato paste
1	large yellow onion, roughly chopped
3	stalks celery, roughly chopped
	White portion of 1 leek, well washed and roughly chopped
12 cups	water
4 cups	Chicken Broth (see p. 17)
2	bay leaves
6	cracked black peppercorns
8	sprigs fresh thyme
10	parsley stems
4	cloves garlic, roughly chopped

(continued on page 178)

(continued from page 176)

Preheat an oven to 500 degrees.

Rub the veal bones with a little olive oil. Place the bones on a large baking sheet with raised sides and put it on the top shelf of the oven. Roast the bones for 30 to 35 minutes, or until a nice dark golden color is obtained. Remove the pan from the oven. Reduce the heat to 450 degrees. Using a rubber spatula or wooden spoon, smear the bones with the tomato paste. Add the chopped vegetables to the bones and return the pan to the oven. Continue to roast for another 30 minutes.

Remove the bones and vegetables from the oven. Put them all into a large stockpot. Take a little of the water and deglaze the baking sheet, scraping the bottom to get all the little bits of brown drippings and vegetables. Add to the stockpot. Add the rest of the water, the chicken broth, bay leaves, peppercorns, thyme, parsley stems, and garlic to the stockpot. If the water does not completely cover the bones, add enough to cover.

Slowly bring the stock just to a boil, and then reduce it to a simmer. It is important not to boil the stock because boiling will make it cloudy. Turn the stock down to a simmer. Skim off the foam that appears on the top and any excessive amounts of fat and discard. Simmer the stock for 4 1/2 to 5 hours. It should have a good flavor and color. Strain, pressing all of the juices out of the vegetables. Discard the solids. Let cool and refrigerate until ready to use.

When stock has been chilled, the fat will solidify at the top and can easily be removed and discarded. You should have an end product of 1 1/2 quarts of veal stock with fat removed.

Madeira Sauce

For an ordinary household, this labor intensive reduction sauce is quite a culinary achievement. However, it is well worth the effort when you want an outstanding sauce to accompany a fine piece of meat or poultry. Make the Veal Stock recipe, then you'll be ready to start the sauce. It is important not to add any salt during the cooking process because salt will concentrate as the liquids are reduced and an over-salted sauce will result.

Makes 1 pint

1 1/2 quarts	Veal Stock (see p. 176)
1 tablespoon	light olive oil
1 cup	roughly chopped yellow onion
1 tablespoon	roughly chopped garlic
2 cups	roughly chopped tomatoes, with juice and seeds
1/4 cup	chopped parsley stems
1 cup	red wine, of drinking quality
1 cup	Madeira wine
	Salt
	White pepper

Place the veal stock in a clean saucepan and reduce by half over medium heat.

Heat the olive oil in heavy-bottomed saucepan. Add the onion, garlic, tomatoes, and parsley stems and sauté for 1 minute. Add the red wine and Madeira and bring the mixture to a boil. Lower the heat and simmer gently until the liquid is reduced by two-thirds.

Add the reduced veal stock to the rest of the ingredients and continue to reduce by simmering. You will get a nice, dark color and intensified flavor as the liquid reduces by one-third to approximately 2 1/2 cups. Strain the mixture, pressing all of the juices out of the vegetables, then strain again through a fine sieve. Return the sauce to the stove and reduce the volume by another third, skimming off any foam that may come to the top. Season to taste with salt and white pepper and a splash of Madeira, if desired.

Golden-Fried Buttermilk Chicken Breasts

This method of frying chicken breasts also works well if you are making sandwiches. If you remove the skin, the breasts will cook in 7 to 8 minutes. For chicken fingers, remove the skin and cut the meat into strips. Follow the same procedure. The cooking time will only be 3 to 4 minutes.

Here's an important frying tip: If you add too many pieces of chicken at once to the oil, it will lower the temperature of the oil and result in soggy, greasy chicken. A good warning sign of improper frying temperature is a lack of bubbling action. Visible rapid frying bubbles and a sizzling sound mean that you are frying properly. This is actually the moisture and juices of the chicken cooking off in the hot oil, which in turn gives the natural starches and sugars a chance to caramelize.

Serves 4

8 cups	peanut, canola, or vegetable oil for frying
8	(5- to 6-ounce) chicken breasts, skin on, boneless, trimmed of excess fat and cartilage
1 cup	buttermilk
2 tablespoons	Texas Pete sauce
1 teaspoon	freshly ground black pepper
1/2 teaspoon	granulated garlic powder
1/2 teaspoon	granulated onion powder

Lay a piece of plastic wrap over your cutting board. Place each chicken breast on it with the skin-side up. Place a double piece of plastic wrap over the breast and lightly pound the thicker end of the chicken breast with the flat side of a mallet. Do not pound thin. Just firmly tap the breast to give it an equal thickness. This also helps to break some of the muscle fibers so that the chicken breast will cook evenly.

Mix the buttermilk, Texas Pete, pepper, garlic powder, and onion powder in a large bowl. Place the pounded breasts in the bowl and allow them to marinate at least an hour, or overnight in the refrigerator.

Seasoned Flour

2 cups	all-purpose flour
1¹/₂ teaspoons	ground white pepper
2 tablespoons	fine sea salt

Combine all of the ingredients.

Preheat the oil to 360 degrees.

Remove the breasts from the marinade and coat them in the seasoned flour mixture. This is an important step because the moisture of the marinade absorbs a little of the flour, which creates a simple spicy batter. Be sure that the entire outside of the breast is coated with flour.

Carefully place the breasts in the heated oil all at the same time so that they cook at the same rate. How many you can do at once depends on how large your fryer is. Three to four pieces at a time works well. As the chicken cooks, gently turn and rotate the pieces occasionally so that they brown evenly, especially if using one of the smaller fryers. Allow the chicken to cook for 10 to 12 minutes, or until golden brown and crispy.

Remove the breasts and place them on paper towels. Season with additional salt to taste. Serve immediately or hold in a 200-degree oven to keep warm if doing large batches.

Chicken and Andouille Gumbo

with Carolina Aromatic Rice

It is very important that the roux is cooked long and slow and allowed to toast to a very dark rich color without burning. This gives this dish its unique nutty flavor and dark rich color. The okra and filé powder actually give this gumbo its consistency, as the thickening capabilities of the roux are lost when it is cooked to this extensive dark state.

Prepare all of the vegetables and spices before beginning to make the roux.

Makes 12 (8-ounce) servings

1 pound	boneless, skinless chicken thighs
6 tablespoons	peanut or canola oil
1/2 cup	all-purpose flour
3/4 cup	diced celery
1 cup	diced onion
1/2 cup	diced red bell pepper
1/2 cup	diced green bell pepper
1 pound	andouille sausage or a good smoked sausage, diced
1/4 cup	tomato paste
1 tablespoon	minced garlic
1 tablespoon	minced fresh thyme
1/2 tablespoon	filé powder
1/2 teaspoon	red pepper flakes
1	bay leaf
5 cups	chicken broth, room temperature
1 tablespoon	fine sea salt
1 1/2 teaspoons	freshly ground black pepper
	Pinch of cayenne pepper
1 1/2 cups	sliced fresh okra, cut in 1/2-inch slices
2 tablespoons	chopped fresh parsley
1/4 cup	sliced scallions
	Carolina Aromatic Rice (see p. 95)

Preheat an oven to 375 degrees.

Place the chicken thighs on a baking sheet with raised sides. Roast for 30 to 40 minutes. Remove from oven and cool. Dice and reserve.

Meanwhile, in a heavy-bottomed pot, heat the oil over medium-high heat until it just begins to smoke. Carefully add the flour all at once and stir with a wooden spoon. Carefully continue to stir the roux for the next 8 to 10 minutes. Move the entire pan on and off the heat to control a slow, even toasting of the flour. A light mahogany color is optimum. If the flour seems to be burnt, discard it and start over. This roux becomes extremely hot, so be very careful.

When the desired color is obtained, lower the heat to medium and remove the pot from the burner. Carefully add the celery, onion, and bell peppers all at once to stop the roux from continuing to brown. Mix the vegetables and roux for 2 minutes, allowing the steam that is produced to be released.

Place the pot back over medium heat and add the sausage, tomato paste, garlic, thyme, filé powder, red pepper flakes, and bay leaf. Stir over medium heat for 2 to 3 minutes, or until the vegetables become soft. Add the chicken broth and whisk vigorously. Bring gradually to a boil, skim off the foam and discard. Continue to cook the gumbo slowly for 7 minutes, stirring occasionally. Add the chicken, salt, pepper, and cayenne pepper. Continue to cook the gumbo over low heat for 6 minutes. During this process oil will rise to the top; skim off the oil and discard. Add the okra and parsley and allow the okra to cook gently in the gumbo for 10 to 15 minutes, or until it stops floating. Too much movement will break up the okra. Discard the bay leaf.

Serve by placing 1 cup of gumbo in each bowl and adding 1/4 cup of the rice in the center. Garnish with the scallions and a sprinkle of filé powder.

Pan-Fried Chicken Livers

with Caramelized Onions, Country Ham, and Madeira Sauce

I have to say, this is the best chicken liver dish in the South. The crispy pan-fried livers with the salty country ham, sweet caramelized onions, and rich Madeira Sauce makes for a combination unlike any other.

Serves 4

3 tablespoons	light olive oil
2 cups	thinly sliced yellow onions, cut in 1/4-inch slices
1 pound	chicken livers
1/2 cup	all-purpose flour
1 teaspoon	salt
1 teaspoon	freshly ground black pepper
6 ounces	country ham, sliced very thin
1 recipe	Madeira Sauce (see p. 179)

Heat 1 tablespoon olive oil in a heavy-bottomed frying pan over high heat until the oil is smoking. Lay the onion slices in the hot oil. You want to keep the slices intact and not loosen them into rings until after the initial searing. Sear for 1 or 2 minutes without turning to start the caramelization process. Cook, tossing occasionally, until the onions caramelize and turn golden brown. At this point, the slices may break into rings. Watch the heat and reduce it slightly if it appears that the onions are beginning to burn. A teaspoon of olive oil can be added if the pan becomes too dry and the bottom begins to scorch. When the onions have browned, remove them from the heat until ready to serve.

Preheat an oven to 350 degrees.

Trim any fat or sinew from the chicken livers. Combine the flour, salt, and pepper, mixing well. Dust the livers with the flour mixture, making certain to cover them completely. Shake off excess flour so that it does not burn in the pan.

Heat the remaining olive oil in a heavy-bottomed frying pan over medium-high heat. Gently place the livers in the hot oil. They will spit and splatter in the oil. Cover with a lid or splatter guard. Sauté on one side for 1 to 2 minutes, or until golden. Uncover the pan, flip the livers over, and continue to cook. If all of the oil has been absorbed, add a little more, a teaspoon at a time.

Put the livers in the oven for 3 to 4 minutes, or until they are firm and their centers are cooked through. While the livers are cooking, sauté the ham in a heavy-bottomed frying pan over medium heat until the ham edges curl up. Add the caramelized onions to the frying pan with the ham and reheat.

When ready to serve, remove the livers from the oven. Place the livers and ham on the plates. Mound the onions in the center. Spoon the Madeira Sauce around the ham, liver, and onions. Serve immediately.

Magnolias' Veal Meatloaf

with Butter-Whipped Potatoes, Mushroom and Sage Gravy, and Tobacco Onions

If you prefer to grill the meatloaf, allow the loaves to cool completely, cut them into 1¼-inch-thick slices, brush the slices lightly with oil, and grill until heated through. This method gives an added grilled flavor. The meatloaf also freezes very well after it is fully cooked and cooled. Just thaw to room temperature before reheating in the oven or grilling.

Serves 6 to 8

Meatloaf

2 tablespoons	light olive oil
2 cups	minced yellow onions
2 tablespoons	minced garlic
1½ tablespoons	minced fresh sage
1½ tablespoons	minced fresh oregano
2 tablespoons	minced fresh parsley
2 pounds	finely ground veal, very well chilled
1¼ pounds	ground pork or bacon, very well chilled
2	eggs, lightly beaten and chilled
4 tablespoons	heavy cream
1 tablespoon	salt
1 teaspoon	freshly ground black pepper

Heat the olive oil in a small heavy-bottomed saucepan. Add the onion and cook until translucent. Add the garlic, sage, oregano, and parsley. Cook 2 minutes, stirring. Remove from the heat and spread out on a plate or pan. Cool to room temperature and refrigerate to cool completely. Reserve.

Place the chilled veal and pork in a mixing bowl and mix together just to combine. Add the chilled onion and herb mixture, the eggs, cream, salt, and pepper. Mix together until well combined. Place the mixture back into the refrigerator to chill.

Preheat an oven to 375 degrees.

Form the meatloaf mixture into two loaves about 4 inches wide, 1½ inches tall, and 10 inches long on a baking sheet with raised sides or use standard loaf pans. Bake for 45 to 50 minutes, or until they reach an internal temperature of 170 degrees. Remove from the oven and allow to rest for 5 minutes before slicing and serving.

Mushroom and Sage Gravy

Makes 3 cups

3 tablespoons	butter
3 tablespoons	minced yellow onion
2 cups	sliced and roughly chopped assorted mushrooms (shiitake, crimini, portobello, morel, chanterelle)

<pre>
  1 teaspoon   minced garlic
 2 teaspoons   chopped fresh sage
     1/4 cup   all-purpose flour
  2 1/2 cups   Chicken Broth (see p. 17)
               Salt
               Freshly ground black pepper
</pre>

Heat the butter. Add the onion, mushrooms, garlic, and sage. Cook over medium-high heat for 3 to 4 minutes, or until the mushrooms are tender and most of their juices have cooked off. Add the flour and stir until combined. Add half the broth and whisk vigorously until the mixture thickens. Add the remaining broth and bring back up to a boil. Skim off any foam that may appear and discard. Cook the gravy for 8 to 10 minutes, or until the gravy is smooth and the starchy flavor of the roux is cooked out. Season to taste with salt and pepper. Keep warm.

Tobacco Onions

<pre>
4 cups   vegetable oil
2 cups   thinly sliced rings of yellow onions, cut into 1/16 inch thick
</pre>

Preheat the oil to 340 degrees in a heavy saucepan with deep sides.

Place the onions in the heated oil and stir gently with a skimmer so that they cook evenly.

As they begin to become golden brown and caramelized, lift them out of the oil, shake off the excess, and place them on paper towels to cool. The onions will continue to cook for a moment.

To finish:

<pre>
Butter-Whipped Potatoes (see p. 93)
Sprigs of fresh sage
</pre>

Place 1/2 cup of the potatoes in the center of each plate and place two pieces of the baked or grilled meatloaf next to the potatoes. Spoon the Mushroom and Sage Gravy over the meatloaf and potatoes and garnish with the Tobacco Onions and a sprig of sage.

Pan-Roasted Chicken Breast

with Crispy Collard and Cabbage Rolls, Lady Peas, Carolina Ham Cracklings, Butter-Whipped Potatoes, and Fried Collards

This dish uses many truly Southern ingredients. I prefer to serve the chicken with the skin on because it protects the tender breast meat while cooking and also renders down to a flavorful golden brown crust. If lady peas are not available, feel free to substitute butter beans, black-eyed peas, or zipper peas. The fried collards have a unique earthy flavor that I associate with nori, the seaweed sheets that are roasted and used for sushi. They make a great garnish and elevate Down South cooking to new heights.

Lumpia wrappers are a lighter, crispier version of egg roll wrappers. They are very thin sheets and generally come frozen. When lumpia wrappers are rolled around a filling and deep-fat fried, they will have a crispy multi-layered golden brown crust.

Serves 4

4	(4- to 5-ounce) chicken breasts, boneless but with the skin on
4 tablespoons	light olive oil
1 tablespoon	coarse sea salt
1 teaspoon	freshly ground black pepper
3 tablespoons	butter
	Butter-Whipped Potatoes (see p. 93)
	Lady Peas (see p. 103)
	Carolina Ham Cracklings (see p. 22)

Trim the chicken breasts of any cartilage and fat, still leaving the skin attached. Heat the oil in a heavy-bottomed pan. Season the chicken breasts with the salt and pepper on all sides. Place them in the oil skin-side down and sear them over medium-high heat. After 1 minute, gently lift the breasts and move the pan to get some of the hot oil under the skin and prevent it from burning. Lower the heat to medium. The goal is to slowly caramelize the skin to a nice golden color.

Carefully turn the breast over and continue cooking the opposite side for 1 to 2 minutes or until it is firm to the touch. Add the butter and allow it to melt and slowly brown, while tilting the pan and spoon-basting the breasts with the oil and butter mixture. Slowly cook for 6 to 7 minutes per side, depending on the size of the breasts, or until cooked through. Remove from the heat and allow to rest in a warm area for 2 to 3 minutes before serving.

Crispy Collard and Cabbage Rolls

Makes 4 rolls

1/2 cup	finely chopped smoked bacon
1/2 cup	sliced yellow onion
3 cups	thinly sliced collard green leaves, washed, stemmed, and cut into 1/8-inch slices, divided
2 cups	thinly sliced cabbage, cut in 1/8-inch slices
2 teaspoons	minced garlic
1 1/2 teaspoons	salt
	White pepper
	Freshly ground black pepper
1 tablespoon	cornstarch
1 tablespoon	water
1 package	lumpia wrappers, thawed
1/2 gallon	canola or peanut oil

In a large heavy pot or wok, cook the bacon over medium heat for 1 minute. Increase the heat to high, add the onions, 2 cups of the collards, and the cabbage. Stir-fry for 1 1/2 minutes, add the garlic, and continue to stir for 1 minute, or until the collards just begin to wilt. Add the salt and the peppers.

Immediately transfer the mixture to a baking sheet and spread out to cool to room temperature. Refrigerate until cold. This can be done a day or two ahead.

Mix the cornstarch and water. Place two lumpia wrappers on a clean counter. Place 1/4 of the filling along the bottom of each wrapper and begin to roll up, keeping them evenly filled and tightly rolled. As you get to the last 1 1/2 inches of each roll, brush with a little of the cornstarch mixture to seal. Continue to roll, and place seam side down on a piece of wax or parchment paper. Repeat until you have 4 rolls. These may be covered and frozen at this point for future use. If the rolls are frozen it is best to let them sit a few minutes at room temperature before frying.

Preheat the oil to 350 degrees.

Gently place the rolls in the heated oil and fry for 2 minutes, or until the ends are golden brown and the rolls are crispy. Remove and place on paper towels. Keep warm. These should be served within 10 minutes to be at their best.

Fried Collards

Preheat the oil to 320 degrees.

Gently place the remaining collard greens in the hot oil. Very gently agitate with a hand skimmer and cook until the bubbles begin to dissipate. Remove the greens, shake off the excess oil, and place on paper towels. Be careful because these will continue to cook after they are removed from the hot oil. Allow to cool to room temperature. These can be done up to 3 to 4 hours ahead.

To finish:

Butter-Whipped Potatoes (see p. 93)
Lady Peas (see p. 103)

Place 1/2 cup potatoes in the center of the plates. Trim the ends of the cabbage and collard rolls and cut into two pieces that are even lengths. Place the two rolls on the potatoes and spoon the lady peas around. Sprinkle with a tablespoon of the ham cracklings and place a chicken breast on top. Garnish with the fried collard greens and serve immediately.

Southern Sweets

Magnolias

Coconut Cream Pie

with Banana Custard Sauce and Caramelized Bananas

This is a favorite for all coconut lovers. The Banana Custard Sauce gives this coconut treat an even more intense tropical flavor. The Caramelized Bananas make for a sweet crunchy garniture.

1 9-inch pie or 8 tartlets

Coconut Cream Filling

1 cup	sugar
1/2 cup	cornstarch
1 1/2 teaspoons	powdered gelatin
1/2 teaspoon	salt
1/2 cup	coconut milk
3	egg yolks, lightly beaten
2 1/2 cups	milk
1/2 teaspoon	almond extract
1 teaspoon	pure vanilla extract
1 1/2 cups	shredded coconut

Combine the sugar, cornstarch, gelatin, and salt in a large bowl. Whisk thoroughly. Add the coconut milk and egg yolks and stir to combine.

Heat the milk in a heavy-bottomed saucepan over medium heat until there are small bubbles around the edges. Slowly pour the hot milk into the egg yolk mixture, whisking constantly. Pour the mixture back into the saucepan. Cook over medium heat, stirring constantly, for about 3 minutes, or until very thick. Remove from the heat. Stir in the extracts and coconut. Allow mixture to cool completely in an ice bath, stirring frequently. Use when cooled or put in a storage container, cover, and refrigerate overnight in the refrigerator.

Short Dough

2 (9-inch) pie shells

³/₄ cup	sugar
³/₄ cup	butter
4 cups	White Lily all-purpose flour
1¹/₂ teaspoons	salt
2	eggs, lightly beaten

Cream the sugar and butter together until light. Add the flour and salt and mix until just combined. Add the eggs and mix until just combined. Roll out on a floured surface until about ³/₁₆ inch thick and larger around than the pie tin or tart shell. Gently roll the dough onto the rolling pin and place in the pie tin. Trim off the edges, leaving enough dough attached to make a nice crimped edge. Place in the refrigerator and chill until firm.

Preheat an oven to 350 degrees.

When ready to bake, pierce the bottom of the crust a few times with the tip of a knife. Place the pie tin on a baking sheet and bake it for 12 to 15 minutes, or until it is a light golden color, rotating the pan 180 degrees halfway through. If the pastry dough "domes" on the bottom, gently press it down with a kitchen towel when rotating the pan. Remove from the oven and cool to room temperature. Add the coconut custard and refrigerate.

Cream Topping

¹/₂ teaspoon	powdered gelatin
1 tablespoon	cold water
1¹/₂ cups	heavy cream
2 tablespoons	sugar
¹/₂ teaspoon	coconut extract

Sprinkle the gelatin over the water and heat the water to melt the gelatin. Place the cream in a mixing bowl with the whip attached. Sprinkle in the sugar. As the cream begins to whip, drizzle in the gelatin and coconut extract. Spread over the custard and refrigerate the pie.

Helpful Hint: Because there is gelatin in this cream to stabilize it, you must place it on the pie before the gelatin sets as it chills. Have the pie ready for this step before making the cream.

Banana Custard Sauce

Makes 2 $\frac{1}{4}$ cups

5	egg yolks
$\frac{1}{2}$	cup sugar
2 cups	heavy cream
$\frac{1}{2}$	vanilla bean, split lengthwise or 1 teaspoon pure vanilla extract
1 teaspoon	banana flavoring

Whisk together the egg yolks and sugar. Put the cream and vanilla bean in a heavy-bottomed saucepan and heat until little bubbles form around the edges. Slowly pour the hot cream into the egg yolk mixture, whisking constantly. Pour the mixture back into the saucepan. Gently cook over medium heat, stirring constantly, until the sauce coats the back of a wooden spoon. Strain into a container. Take out the vanilla bean and scrape the vanilla bean seeds from the pod into the custard. Discard the vanilla bean. Add the banana flavoring and cool immediately in an ice bath. When cool, cover and refrigerate. Serve cold.

Caramelized Bananas

2	bananas
$\frac{1}{2}$ cup	sugar

Slice the bananas on the bias about $\frac{3}{8}$ inch thick and place on a baking sheet. Sprinkle with the sugar and use a self-igniting propane torch to caramelize the sugar. This should be done just prior to serving.

Cut the pie into 8 to 10 slices and serve with a small amount of the banana custard sauce and 2 to 3 pieces of the caramelized bananas.

Sweet Biscuit

with Fresh Strawberries, Whipped Cream, and Orange Custard Sauce

Makes 8 (2 1/2-inch) biscuits

7	tablespoons cold diced salted butter
2 cups plus 2 tablespoons	White Lily all-purpose flour
7 tablespoons	sugar
1 tablespoon	aluminum-free baking powder
3/4 teaspoon	salt
1/2 cup	buttermilk
2 tablespoons	heavy cream

Preheat an oven to 375 degrees.

Dice the butter, put it on a plate, and place it in the refrigerator to remain cold while assembling the other ingredients. Combine the flour, 3 tablespoons sugar, the baking powder, and salt. Add the diced butter and cut into the flour with either a pastry cutter or two forks until the mixture is crumbly.

Add the buttermilk a little at a time until the dough comes together and forms a ball. Place it on a floured surface, sprinkle it with flour, and pat it out to a 1-inch-thick circle. Cut the biscuits with a 2 1/2-inch biscuit cutter and place them on a heavy baking sheet. Brush the tops of the biscuits with cream and sprinkle heavily with remaining sugar.

Place the baking sheet on the middle shelf of the oven and bake for 15 to 20 minutes. Remove and cool to room temperature.

Strawberries

| 2 pints | strawberries, washed, stemmed, and sliced |
| 2 tablespoons | sugar |

When ready to serve the biscuits, toss the sliced strawberries with the sugar and let them sit for 5 minutes before plating them. The combination of the sugars and the natural juices of the strawberries will produce a nice strawberry syrup.

Whipped Cream

1 cup	heavy cream
1½ tablespoons	sugar
¼ teaspoon	pure vanilla extract

Place the cold cream in a chilled mixing bowl. Whip in the sugar slowly and add the vanilla. Continue to whip until the cream has tripled in volume and is firm, yet creamy.

Split the biscuits and place the bottom half on each plate. Spoon the strawberries over the bottom halves, add a dollop of whipped cream and replace the tops. Spoon Orange Custard Sauce (see p. 204) around the edges.

Magnolias' Baked Creams

with Orange Custard Sauce

This is the custard lover's custard. It doesn't have the caramelized sugar syrup that classically accompanies it. We prefer the Orange Custard Sauce. The milk in the baked creams is infused with fresh orange zest so that they also have a subtle orange flavor. I like to garnish them with orange segments, strawberries, and blueberries.

To take the zest off of citrus fruits, use a zester or a microplane, which removes a thinner layer of the zest.

Makes 8 creams

4 cups	milk
1¹/₂ cups	sugar, divided
¹/₂	vanilla bean, split lengthwise or 1 teaspoon pure vanilla extract
	Zest of 1 orange, roughly chopped
6	eggs
4	egg yolks
	Fresh fruit to garnish

Preheat an oven to 300 degrees. You will need 8 (6-ounce) ramekins or heatproof custard cups and a roasting pan with deep sides large enough to hold them.

Place the milk, ³/₄ cup sugar, the vanilla bean, and the orange zest in a heavy-bottomed saucepan over medium heat. Slowly bring the mixture to a boil. Remove the mixture from the heat and strain. Scrape the inside of the vanilla bean, putting the seeds back into the hot milk. Discard the vanilla bean and the orange zest.

In a separate bowl, beat the eggs, egg yolks, and the remaining sugar together until combined. Slowly stream the hot milk mixture into the egg mixture, stirring continuously. When half of the milk is incorporated into the egg mixture, slowly pour the mixture back into the pan of hot milk, stirring continuously.

Pour the mixture into the 8 ramekins and sit them in the roasting pan. Place the pan on the middle shelf of the oven. Pull the shelf out and add enough hot water to the pan to come halfway up the sides of the ramekins, making sure, however, not to get any water into the creams. This "water bath" deflects the direct heat, which would cook the outsides of the creams before the insides finish cooking.

Bake the creams for approximately 1 hour and 40 minutes, carefully rotating the pan 180 degrees halfway through baking, or until the creams are firm. A knife inserted into the center of one of the creams should come out without any milky liquid on it. Pull out the rack carefully and lift out the creams with towels or a slotted heavy spatula. Place on a rack to cool to room temperature and discard the water bath.

Chill the creams for 4 hours or overnight. Gently run a knife around the inside edges of the ramekins. Unmold the creams on individual dessert plates. Serve with Orange Custard Sauce and garnish with fresh fruit.

Orange Custard Sauce

You'll find many ways to use this sauce. It goes especially well with dense, rich chocolate desserts.

Makes 2 cups

2 cups	heavy cream
1/2 cup	sugar
	Zest of 1/2 orange
1/4	vanilla bean, split lengthwise, or 1/2 teaspoon pure vanilla extract
5	egg yolks

Place the cream in a heavy-bottomed saucepan with half the sugar, the orange zest, and vanilla bean. In a separate bowl, beat the egg yolks with the other half of the sugar until combined. Heat the cream over medium heat until there are small bubbles around the edges. Slowly stream the hot cream into the egg yolk mixture, stirring constantly. When half the cream is incorporated into the egg mixture, slowly pour the mixture back into the pan of hot cream, stirring continuously.

Place the pan over low heat and, stirring constantly with a wooden spoon, cook the custard until it is thick enough to coat the back of the spoon. Strain into a container. Take out the vanilla bean and scrape the vanilla bean seeds from the pod into the custard. Discard the vanilla bean and the orange zest. Cool immediately in an ice bath. Cover and refrigerate. Serve cold.

Orange Custard Sauce will keep in the refrigerator for 2 to 3 days.

Warm Cream Cheese Brownie

with Vanilla Bean Ice Cream, and Chocolate and Caramel Sauces

Days before finalizing our first dessert menu at Magnolias, I sampled one of these at Nancy Smith's house. It was typical of her simple ideas and warm hospitality. The brownies are great alone, but we dress them up with ice cream and chocolate and caramel sauces. Cream cheese brownies won't be forgotten in the Barickman family because they also provided a perfect surprise hiding place for my wife's engagement ring.

Makes 24 brownies

Cream Cheese Batter

6 ounces	cream cheese, room temperature
4 tablespoons	unsalted butter, room temperature
1/2 cup	sugar
2	eggs
1 teaspoon	pure vanilla extract
2 tablespoons	White Lily all-purpose flour
1/2 cup	semisweet chocolate chips

Beat the cream cheese, butter, and sugar until well blended. Add the eggs one at a time, beating well and scraping down the sides of the bowl at least once. Beat in the vanilla. Fold in the flour and chips and set aside.

Preheat an oven to 325 degrees.

Using vegetable shortening, grease a 9 x 13-inch pan, line it with foil, and grease the foil.

Chocolate Batter

4 ounces	unsweetened chocolate
4 ounces	semisweet chocolate
6 tablespoons	unsalted butter
4	eggs

(continued on page 207)

(continued from page 205)

1 1/2 cups	sugar
2 teaspoons	pure vanilla extract
1 cup	White Lily all-purpose flour
2 teaspoons	aluminum-free baking powder
1 teaspoon	salt
1 cup	semisweet chocolate chips

Melt the chocolate and butter in a double boiler or over very low heat. Remove from the heat and cool to room temperature. Beat the eggs, gradually adding the sugar, until the eggs are thick and light in color. Blend in the cooled chocolate mixture. Add the vanilla and combine well.

Combine the flour, baking powder, and salt and fold into the chocolate mixture. Fold in the chocolate chips. Spoon the chocolate batter into the greased baking pan. Spread the cream cheese batter in 1-inch-thick lines on top of the chocolate batter. Use a knife tip to pull the dark and light batters together by dragging the tip back and forth.

Bake the brownies for 35 to 40 minutes, or until a cake tester comes out clean. The edges of the brownies will have puffed, but the center will still be fairly soft. The center will firm up, however, because it will continue to cook after the pan is removed from the oven. Cool the brownies in the pan before cutting. They should be very rich and moist.

Chocolate Sauce

Makes 1 3/4 cups

1 cup	heavy cream
1/2 pound	semisweet chocolate

It doesn't matter whether you use chopped blocks of chocolate or chocolate chips as long as you use a good quality chocolate, preferably on the dark side.

Bring the cream to a boil in a heavy-bottomed saucepan over medium heat. Place the chocolate in a mixing bowl and add the boiling cream, whisking continuously until chocolate has melted and the sauce is smooth. Use at once or cool to room temperature, pour into storage container, cover, and refrigerate. The sauce keeps for 2 weeks in the refrigerator.

Caramel Sauce

Makes 1½ cups

8 tablespoons	unsalted butter
1 cup	light brown sugar
½ cup	cream
½ teaspoon	pure vanilla extract
	Dash of salt

Melt the butter and sugar in a heavy-bottomed saucepan and stir over medium heat until the sugar is completely dissolved and the mixture is thick and bubbly. Slowly add the cream in small amounts, stirring constantly. Add the vanilla and salt and bring the mixture to a boil, stirring. Remove the caramel from the heat. Use at once or cool to room temperature, pour into a storage container, cover, and refrigerate. The caramel keeps for 2 weeks in the refrigerator. Both the chocolate and the caramel sauces can be rewarmed by stirring them over simmering water in a double boiler or microwaving them very slowly.

Chocolate Chip Pecan Pie
with Bourbon Sauce

This old favorite makes a great addition to a winter dinner menu. In the fall, the plump pecans have just come off of the trees and they bake up crisp. The chocolate and the Bourbon Sauce add to the decadence.

Makes 1 pie

1	(10-inch) piecrust (see p. 24)
4	eggs, room temperature
1/2 cup plus 2 tablespoons	sugar
1 cup	dark corn syrup
1 tablespoon	pure vanilla extract
6 tablespoons	unsalted butter, melted and kept warm
1 1/2 cups	chopped pecans
3/4 cup	semisweet chocolate chips

Preheat an oven to 350 degrees.

Place a heavy baking sheet on the bottom rack of the oven for 5 minutes before putting the pie in the oven. This will provide extra heat to help the bottom crust brown.

Place the eggs, sugar, corn syrup, and vanilla in a bowl and whisk to combine. Scrape the side and bottom of the bowl at least twice while mixing. Add the warm butter. Mix well. Combine the pecans and chocolate chips and sprinkle them on the bottom of the pie shell. Pour the filling over the nuts and chips.

Place the pie on the baking sheet on the bottom shelf of the oven and bake for 30 minutes. Move the pie to the middle shelf and continue to bake it for another 15 to 20 minutes. The edges of the filling will rise, but the middle will still be a little bouncy. However, the pie will continue to bake after it is removed from the oven. To have it firm enough to slice, allow the pie to cool for 2 to 3 hours.

You may serve the pie as is or add vanilla ice cream or Bourbon Sauce.

Bourbon Sauce

Makes 2 cups

1 cup	diced unsalted butter
1 cup plus 2 tablespoons	firmly packed dark brown sugar
1/2 cup	heavy cream
1/4 cup	bourbon

Melt the butter and sugar in a heavy-bottomed saucepan over medium heat, whisking continuously for 5 to 10 minutes, or until the sugar is completely dissolved. Slowly whisk in the cream and then the bourbon. Use at once or cool to room temperature, pour into a storage container, cover, and refrigerate. The sauce will keep for 1 week in the refrigerator.

To rewarm the sauce, stir it over simmering water in a double boiler or over low heat. If the heat is too high, the sauce may separate.

Magnolias' Berry Cobbler

Another way to enjoy the summer berries. The crunchy sweet golden brown topping is the way I like my cobbler, especially with ice cream. Try it with fresh peaches when they are available.

Serves 8 to 10

Filling

6 cups	fresh blueberries
3 cups	fresh strawberries
1 1/2 cups	sugar
1 tablespoon	fresh lemon juice
1/2 cup	White Lily all-purpose flour
1/2 teaspoon	salt

Combine the berries, sugar, lemon juice, flour, and salt, tossing the fruit until the other ingredients coat it. Pour the fruit into a 9 x 13-inch baking pan.

Topping

6 tablespoons	cold, diced salted butter
1 1/2 cups	White Lily all-purpose flour
1/2 cup	sugar
1/2 teaspoon	aluminum-free baking powder
1/2 teaspoon	salt
1/4 cup plus 1 tablespoon	buttermilk

Preheat an oven to 350 degrees.

Refrigerate the butter while assembling the other ingredients. Combine the flour, sugar, baking powder, and salt and stir to mix well. Add the diced butter and cut it into the flour with either a pastry cutter or two forks until the mixture is crumbly. Add the buttermilk a little at a time until the dough starts to come together. However, this dough should not form a ball like pie dough does. The topping should still be very crumbly, and not sticky. Sprinkle the topping over the filling. It should be about 1/2 inch thick.

Bake the cobbler in the middle of the oven for 1 hour, or until the topping is a light golden color and the berry filling is bubbling up around the sides. Remove the cobbler from the oven and let it cool for a few minutes. Serve with ice cream or whipped cream.

Vanilla Crème Brulée

It is very important not to overcook these custards; if they cook too fast, the custard will steam or soufflé and an undesirable grainy texture will result. They must cook slowly and evenly to be silky and smooth. Even though self-igniting torches are more expensive, I strongly recommend them. The less expensive ones will lose their flame when inverted to burn the sugar, a crucial step for a successful crème Brulée.

Serves 4

3 cups	heavy cream
3/4 cup	sugar
1/2	vanilla bean, split lengthwise
10	egg yolks

Preheat an oven to 285 degrees.

Place the cream in a heavy-bottomed saucepan with half the sugar and the vanilla bean. In a separate bowl, beat the egg yolks with the other half of the sugar until combined. Heat the cream over medium until there are small bubbles around the edges. Slowly stream the hot cream into the egg yolk mixture, stirring constantly. When half the cream is incorporated into the egg mixture, slowly pour the mixture back into the pan of hot cream, stirring constantly. Strain into a container and scrape the vanilla bean seeds from the pod into the cream. Discard the pod. Skim off any foam and place the mixture in an ice bath to chill.

Pour the mixture into 4 brulée dishes or ramekins and place them in a roasting pan with deep sides. Place the pan on the middle shelf of the oven. Pull the shelf out and add enough hot water to the pan to come halfway up the sides of the dishes, making sure not to get any water into the dishes. This water bath deflects the direct heat, which would cook the outsides of the custards before the insides finish cooking. Gently slide the rack back into the oven. Bake the custards for approximately 40 to 45 minutes, carefully rotating the pan 180 degrees halfway through baking.

When the custards are set, pull out the rack carefully and lift them out with towels or a slotted heavy spatula. Place on a rack to cool to room temperature and discard the water bath. Chill the custards for 4 hours or overnight.

Brulée Topping

1/2 cup   granulated white sugar
           Self-igniting propane torch

When ready to serve, gently pat the surface of the custards with a clean towel to eliminate any condensation that may have accumulated. Sprinkle a light layer of sugar on them and burn the tops directly with the propane torch to caramelize the sugar and lightly burn the cream. A few additions of sugar are necessary as the sugar begins to caramelize. Serve immediately.

Summer Berries with Grand Marnier and Brown Sugar Sabayon

This is a great simple way to literally "whip" up a sauce at the last minute. You can even experiment with different flavored liquors, sugars, or citrus for interesting combinations. If chilled before serving, it will lose about one-third of its volume.

Serves 4

6	egg yolks
¼ cup	light brown sugar
2 tablespoons	Grand Marnier liqueur
1 teaspoon	orange zest
2 pints	strawberries, blueberries, raspberries, or blackberries, or a combination, rinsed with cold water and dried on paper towels

Place a saucepan of water over medium-high heat. Combine the egg yolks, brown sugar, Grand Marnier, and orange zest in a stainless bowl. Set the bowl on top of the saucepan. Whisk the mixture vigorously with a whip for 3 to 4 minutes, or until the mixture triples in volume. The temperature should read 140 degrees on an instant-read thermometer. When cooked enough, the sabayon will have a shiny sheen and leave obvious ribbons when the whisk is lifted out. Remove from the heat and serve immediately over the berries or place over ice water and stir occasionally to cool completely, pour into a storage container, cover, and refrigerate.

Mocha Chocolate Mousse
with Whipped Cream

This mousse is only as good as the chocolate that you use, so purchase the best available.

Serves 4

7 ounces	good-quality semisweet chocolate, chopped
3	egg yolks
1/3 cup	honey
2 teaspoons	espresso powder or coffee liqueur
2 cups	heavy cream
	Extra whipped cream for garnish
	Cocoa powder for garnish

Place the chocolate in a stainless bowl and melt over a double boiler. Set aside. Place the yolks in a mixer and whip on medium speed. Put the honey in a very small saucepan and bring to a boil. Remove the foam from the honey and discard it. Slowly pour the hot honey into the whipping yolks. Continue to whip until the yolk mixture has tripled in volume. Fold the egg mixture into the melted chocolate, which has cooled but is still velvety. Place in a large bowl and reserve.

Place the cream in a mixing bowl. Add the espresso powder or liqueur and stir to dissolve. Whip on medium speed until the cream doubles in volume and is smooth and creamy. If you whip the cream too much, the mousse may become grainy in appearance and texture.

Fold half the whipped cream into the chocolate mixture until fully incorporated. Continue with the other half of the whipped cream. Divide the mousse between 4 glasses and refrigerate. You may also pipe or spoon the mousse into Short Dough pastry shells (see p. 198).

Serve with a dollop of whipped cream and a sprinkle of cocoa powder.

Lodge Alley Fig Tartlets with Vanilla Ice Cream

Every year when we see the fig tree in the alley next to Magnolias, it's always a reminder that this wonderful local fruit is on its way to endless creations for its short season. This is just one of those examples.

Makes 4 (3-inch) tartlets

2 pints	fresh figs, rinsed, stems removed
2 tablespoons	butter
¼ cup	light brown sugar
Pinch	fine sea salt
Pinch	ground cloves
½ teaspoon	ground cinnamon, divided
4	(3-inch) Short Dough tart shells (see p. 198), baked just until firm but with no color and still in tart rings
1 tablespoon	sugar
1 cup	vanilla ice cream

Preheat an oven to 350 degrees.

Select the best looking figs and reserve 6 of them. Cut the remaining figs into small wedges until you have 2 cups. Heat the butter in a heavy-bottomed saucepan. Add the brown sugar, stirring to combine. Add the figs, salt, cloves, and ¼ teaspoon ground cinnamon. Cook over medium-low heat for 8 to 10 minutes, or until it reaches jam-like consistency. Remove from the heat and cool to room temperature.

Divide the fig jam equally between the pre-baked tartlet shells. Cut each of the reserved raw figs into wedges and arrange them in a circular fashion on top of the jam, pushing them lightly into it. Mix the remaining cinnamon with the sugar and sprinkle over each tartlet. Bake for 7 to 10 minutes, or until the fig jam begins to bubble and the sugar has melted.

Serve warm with a small scoop of vanilla ice cream.

Resources

Carolina Plantation Aromatic Rice

Carolina Plantation Aromatic Rice
 1515 Mont Clare Road
 P. O. Box 505
 Darlington, South Carolina 29540
 Toll Free (877) 742-3496
 (843) 395-8058
 Fax (843) 395-6769

Products: Aromatic rice, brown rice, rice flour, white and yellow grits, cowpeas

www.carolinaplantationrice.com

White Lily Flour

The White Lily Foods Company
 218 East Depot Street
 Knoxville, Tennessee 37917

www.whitelily.com

Rumford Premium Aluminum-Free Baking Powder

Clabber Girl Corporation
 P.O. Box 150
 Terre Haute, Indiana 47808

www.clabbergirl.com

Stone-Ground White Grits

Falls Mill
 134 Falls Mill Road
 Belvidere, Tennessee 37306
 (931) 469-7161

www.fallsmill.com

Magnolias' Stone-Ground Grits

Magnolias Restaurant
 185 East Bay Street
 Charleston, South Carolina 29401
 (843) 577-7771

www.magnolias-blossom-cypress.com

Carolina Ham Trimmings

Lee's Sausage Company Inc.
 1054 Neeses Highway
 Orangeburg, South Carolina 29115
 (803) 534-5517

Tasso

Local specialty markets, or

www.cajungrocer.com

Nueske's Applewood-Smoked Bacon

Nueske's Hillcrest Farm
 Rural Route 2
 P.O. Box D
 Wittenberg, WI 54499-0904
 (800) 392-2266

www.nueskes.com

Or local specialty markets

Index